The
Year
of the
Poet XII

April 2025

The Poetry Posse

inner child press, ltd.

'building bridges of cultural understanding'

The Poetry Posse 2025

Gail Weston Shazor
Shareef Abdur Rasheed
Teresa E. Gallion
hülya n. yılmaz
Noreen Snyder
Tzemin Ition Tsai
Elizabeth Esguerra Castillo
Jackie Davis Allen
Mutawaf Shaheed
Caroline 'Ceri' Nazareno
Ashok K. Bhargava
Alicja Maria Kuberska
Swapna Behera
Albert 'Infinite' Carrasco
Kimberly Burnham
Eliza Segiet
William S. Peters, Sr.

~ * ~

In order to maintain each poet's authentic voice, this volume has not undergone the scrutiny of editing. Please take time to indulge each contributor for their own creativity and aspirations to convey their uniqueness.

hülya n. yılmaz, Ph.D.
Director of Editing ~
Inner Child Press International

General Information

The Year of the Poet XII
April 2025 Edition

The Poetry Posse

1st Edition : 2025

Publisher Information
1st Edition : Inner Child Press
intouch@innerchildpress.com
www.innerchildpress.com

Copyright © 2025 : The Poetry Posse

ISBN-13 : 978-1-961498-62-4 (inner child press, ltd.)

$ 12.99

WHAT WOULD LIFE BE WITHOUT A LITTLE POETRY?

Dedication

This Book is dedicated to

Humanity, Peace & Poetry

the Power of the Pen

can effectuate change!

&

The Poetry Posse

past, present & future,

our Patrons and Readers &

the Spirit of our Everlasting Muse

In the darkness of my life
I heard the music
I danced . . .
and the Light appeared
and I dance

Janet P. Caldwell

Table of Contents

The Poetry Posse

Table of Contents . . . *continued*

Foreword

Life Ordeals

In all its complexity, life weaves together moments of boundless joy and profound sorrow, resilience and grief, steadfast certainty and relentless self-doubt. To journey through its intricate paths is to face these forces head-on, to grapple with their profound influence, and, if we are fortunate, to emerge with a greater understanding of ourselves and the world.

April is also a month of celebration and dedication through our written unveiled metaphors. This collection of poetry delves into the essence of our shared humanity, exploring the crucible where resilience is shaped amidst grief and tempered by the persistent shadow of self-doubt.

Resilience is often celebrated as an inherent, unyielding force, but in truth, it is an art painstakingly learned. It is not defined by an absence of suffering but by the ability to rise from its depths, to rebuild from shattered fragments, and to navigate forward even in the darkest times. These poems reveal the arduous journey of resilience—the quiet determination that flourishes in the face of adversity. They remind us that resilience is not a single monumental act but a series of micro-steady steps—a refusal to be defined by setbacks.

Grief, an inevitable companion of love and loss, is universal in its reach yet deeply personal in its expression. It is a raw, overwhelming force that leaves us adrift in sorrow's vast seas. Within these pages, grief's complex nature is laid bare—its power to immobilize and to transform, its ability to strip us down and uncover hidden strength. The poets embrace the nonlinear nature of healing, offering glimpses of despair and rays of hope. Through them, we find solace in shared experience, a reminder that no one is truly alone in their pain.

Entwined with resilience and grief is the insidious murmur of self-doubt. This inner voice challenges our worth and undermines our confidence. Self-doubt can be a relentless foe, an ever-present critic sowing seeds of insecurity. Yet, the emotions in these artistic collaborations confront inner struggles with courage, silencing doubts, embracing vulnerability, and nurturing self-compassion.

The Poetry Posse Family here does not aim to instruct on overcoming adversity but stands as living proof to the human spirit's remarkable capacity for endurance. It reflects the intricate interplay between resilience, grief, and self-doubt— a dance that molds our lives and defines our humanity. Born of lived experience, the wisdom embroidered in our poems offers a window into the profound strength of vulnerability, the transformative force of pain, and the enduring resilience that comes from facing our inner fears.

May these creative juices serve as a light in the darkness, a reminder of the human spirit's extraordinary capacity for healing and growth. May they inspire you to embrace your own vulnerability, to nurture resilience through adversity, and to quiet the voices of self-doubt. Within the crucible of being, we discover the unyielding strength of our humanity.

C'est la vie!

Caroline 'Ceri' Nazareno-Gabis

Changing
the
World

one poem at a time

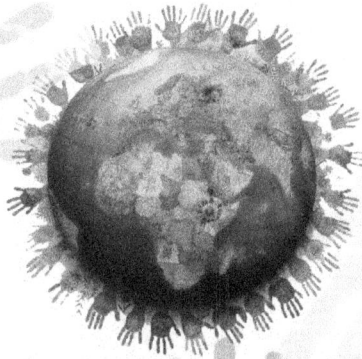

The Conscious Poets

Preface

We, **Inner Child Press International, The Year of the Poet** and **The Poetry Posse** welcome you.

As we now have entered our 12th year of monthly publications for **The Year of the Poet**, we continue to be excited.

This particular year we have chosen to feature a collection of human emotions. We do hope you enjoy the poet's perspectives on these subjects. Read ~ Learn.

For those of you who are not familiar with our story, back in 2013, a few of us poets got together with the simple intention of producing a book a month. That was our challenge. Since that time the enterprise has blossomed and brought forth a fruit that seems to keep on growing as evidenced as we enter 2023.

Our purpose is simple. Through our lyrical words and verse, we not only wish to share our poetic works, but we also have the poetic naiveté to believe that we can assist in the growth of consciousness of the things that have an effect our collective humanity. Therefore, we welcome your readership. For more about what we are attempting to accomplish, have a look at our Publishing Web Site . . . www.innerchildpress.com. If you would like to

know a bit more about this particular endeavor please stop by for a visit at :
www.innerchildpress.com/the-year-of-the-poet

Over the years, Inner Child Press has been socially active to bring awareness and catalog through literature the things that have an impact upon our world and its inhabitants. We have solicited, produced, underwritten and published quite a few volumes to that end. For more insight you may wish to visit : www.innerchildpress.com/the-anthology-market. If you are a writer, poet, or activist, you would be advised to keep a eye out for upcoming volumes should you desire to participate. All readers are welcomed as well. Note, that there is a myriad of published volumes that are available as a FREE PDF download as well as available for purchase at affordable prices.

We at this time extend to you our well wishes for your own personal journey and hope that you consider including us as a travel companion.

Bless Up

Bill

William S. Peters, Sr.

Publisher
Inner Child Press International
www.innerchildpress.com

Resilience, Grief, Self–Doubt

Resilience   Self Doubt   Grief
Calendula   Centaury   Chrysanthemums

The themes for April 2025 The Year of the Poet are Resilience, the ability to recover from adversity; Grief, deep emotional pain during difficult life events or crisis; and Self-Doubt, questioning one's worth or abilities.

On the subject of resilience poet, Lynn Ungar, "Imagine with me for a moment, don't worry, I'm not saying it's real. Imagine, if you can, that there has been not a calamity, but a great awakening ... In this pretty fantasy, everyone who possibly can stops commuting. Spends the extra time with their kids or pets or garden ... The world could never change so radically overnight. But imagine."

In Not to Make Loss Beautiful, Gregory Orr says, "Not to make loss beautiful, But to make loss the place Where beauty starts. Where the heart understands For the first time The nature of its journey."

In an online group, Rosemerry Wahtola Trommer created a group poem, with poets contributing a line or two including, "Grief is ... today grief roots going down into the earth, today grief is full of confusion it's a river of tears the world, today grief is silence that fills the cabinets the couch the car and the driveway ..."

Each of us can create a poem with lines about how grief touches us, when do we feel it?, What reminds us of loss? What can we learn from resilience and grief in our lives.

This month's themes also ask us to consider, "How can we use poetry, reflections, and conversations to overcome self-doubt and shine in the best way we can?"

In Container of Compassion, Sister Steadiness suggests, "my teacher once asked me, how can we package compassion … can we walk all through the day, the evening and the night and allow our fresh hearts to greet each living being? and as we greet the people, animals, plants and minerals along our path, above and below shall we also meet the subtle beings, the mental beings—our thoughts, our feelings, our perceptions and our consciousness with kindness, with warmth, and equanimity and perhaps we may become containers of compassion, parcels of light for each other."

In Why I Write, Anne Marsland suggests another approach, "I write because writing gives me space to reflect, remember, remind, rediscover, relieve … I write because something about coming to the page compels me to be honest with myself. I write because where else can I tell you about the deer that I locked eyes with on the greenway, the two of us frozen and unflinching, all my countless worries suddenly put on pause. Where else can I meander around in the dark, searching for words to say to my fifteen-year-old … I write because life is beautiful and painful, and there is room on the page for it all."

Write your own "Why I Write …" poem.

Kimberly Burnham
Spokane Washington

Poets . . .
sowing seeds in the
Conscious Garden of Life,
that those who have yet to come
may enjoy the Flowers.

Poets, Writers . . . know that we are the enchanting magicians that nourishes the seeds of dreams and thoughts . . . it is our words that entice the hearts and minds of others to believe there is something grand about the possibilities that life has to offer and our words tease it forth into action . . . for you are the Poet, the Writer to whom the Gift of Words has been entrusted . . .

~ wsp

poetry is . . .

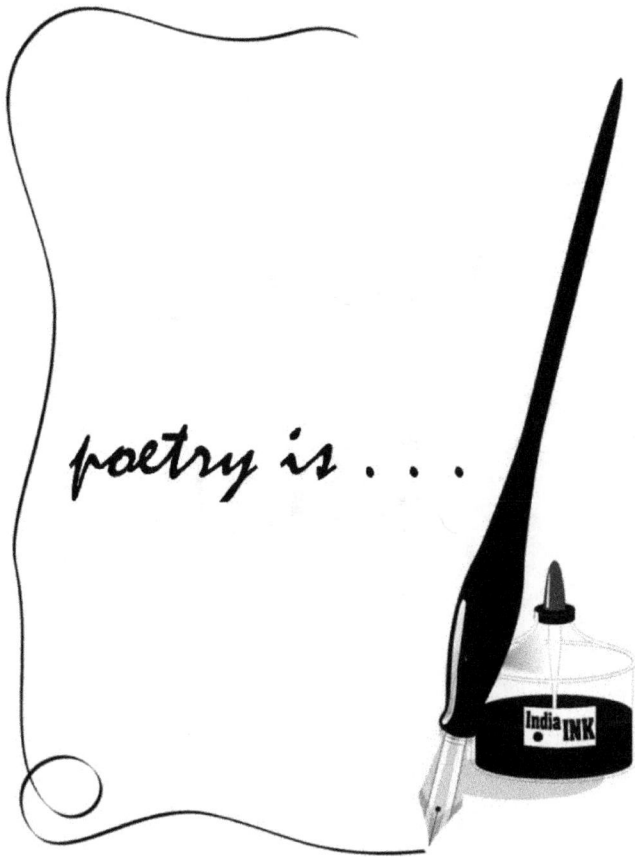

Poetry succeeds where instruction fails.

~ wsp

Coming Soon . . .

Shareef
a soldier for
Allah

Patriarch, Activist & Humanitarian

Friends of the Pen

Gail Weston Shazor

Gail Weston Shazor

Gail Weston Shazor is a lover of words. She is fond of the arcane, unusual and the not yet words.

Coining words at an early age, there was often a bit of trouble with teachers, but she always had her mother and aunt to back up her choices in expression. Born in Mississippi, she spent her early years with her grandparents. Each of the four left very careful influences on her pre-schooling. She learned in turn how women worked in and out of the home and how men worked in and out of the home to support the family. She learned that a lack of proper schooling was not the only way to learn and understanding life was a great teacher. As in most rural families of color, women had a greater chance of formal learning. Both of Gail's grandmothers read out loud to the family whether it was the bible or the newspapers and important documents to their spouses.

Gail Weston Shazor has authored (so far) Notes from the Blue Roof, A Overstanding of an Imperfect Love, HeartSongs and Lies My Grandfather's Told Me. The number of anthologies is too many to list with the premier accomplishment of one of the contributors to The Year of The Poet. Gail will always lend her ink to community projects and will purchase the books of fellow poets in the Inner Child Press family.

A Winter's Tale

We have no snow
Nothing to blanket the sky
Save the rising sun
And still I am chilled
At the possibility of
Cold uncovered limbs
In the quiet of the night

You speak in riddles
That ride upon the west wind
Unresolved whispers
Floating above the heads
Of the unbelievers
And I want to touch the truth
Hiding inside the clouds

I tried to write your name
In my favorite blues
When everyone else
Is wearing the color of goldenrod
I sold a piece of my soul
In the summer of my youth
And the sea has yet to return
The missing to me

Gently, paper lanterns
Light the sky at full noon
I cannot compete with their shine
Even when they are not needed
I stay on my path
And so my limbs are uncovered
Quietly

Dressed/Undressed

I know what you want from me
It is the same thing
Everyone has always wanted
I tried to give it to you all
Time and again
But I failed and not just failed
I bombed it
Wholeheartedly
Because you see it is like this
The me box you fixed for me
Doesn't fit me well
Nor do the me words
You so earnestly want me to speak
And the me thoughts
You say to me convincingly slow
While your eyebrows dance
In the middle of your forehead
Excitedly
It was perhaps mean of me
To play along with the brain washing
But I couldn't interrupt your enjoyment
At the prospect of winning
When all along I already knew
You would wear your surprise
Of my non-conformity
All across your shoulders.
And I would wear it like a gown
Of the finest silk

Oh Death

Death has spared me over yet again
I do not think of death often
I plan my days for the next and the next
Without the thought that it is not promised
For in my small idea of humanity
I am not finished with the dreamtasks
I have stored in my head
And my 51 years are fortunate
The non-discriminatory timeframes
That border our waking and sleeping
Our rest and activity, our praying and praising
 I do not think of death often
I wish to think that it doesn't think of me either
That somewhere the reaper is too busy
To give notion to my threads
And time keeps on moving
Whilst it attends to other tasks of fate
The words come heavy with dry breath
At the mention of death
As if any of us could escape notice
By only whispering its name
Without the fanfare that could draw attention
To what time we have remaining

I hold no notion that I will not die
And when I am forced to think on it
It is always with the thoughts of
Those I will leave to live without me
For even I know that death is for the living
The finality of the last breath
Does nothing for the breather
And the pain ceases with the end of mortality

On this day and in this week
Death has brushed by raising the hairs on my neck
And I realize that I am sad for me
Sad for everyone who feels the touch of ending
Old and young alike, freed from the bondage of dreams
From remembering what it was like to be near
The vibrancy of love and community
No one knows what will happen
Or even when it will happen
But because of this week, we know it will happen
Whether we do or do not think on death often

Gail Weston Shazor

Alicja
Maria
Kuberska

Alicja Maria Kuberska

Alicja Maria Kuberska – awarded Polish poetess, novelist, journalist, editor.

She is a member of the Polish Writers Associations in Warsaw, Poland and IWA Bogdani, Albania. She is also a member of directors' board of Soflay Literature Foundation, Our Poetry Archive (India) and Cultural Ambassador for Poland (Inner Child Press, USA)

Her poems have been published in numerous anthologies and magazines in : Poland, Czech Republic, Slovakia, Hungary,Ukraina, Belgium, Bulgaria, Albania, Spain, the UK, Italy, the USA, Canada, the UK, Argentina, Chile, Peru, Israel, Turkey, India, Uzbekistan, South Korea, Taiwan, China, Australia, South Africa, Zambia, Nigeria

She received two medals - the Nosside UNESCO Competition in Italy (2015) and European Academy of Science Arts and Letters in France (2017). Ahe also received a reward of international literary competition in Italy „ Tra le parole e 'elfinito" (2018). She was announced a poet of the 2017 year by Soflay Literature Foundation (2018).She also received : Bolesław Prus Prize Poland (2019), Culture Animator Poland (2019) and first prize Premio Internazionale di Poesia Poseidonia- Paestrum Italy (2019).

Niobe

People say she is insensitive.
Standing stiffly,
she appears indifferent,
suspended in time
like a spider on a thread.

She is neither shouting nor crying.
Silence surrounds her
and she is cold like a stone.
Only Niobe knows
how it is to be a fossilized pillar.

Autumn Melancholy

Melancholy returned home in November
and it started to live in all the rooms.
It placed dim light in the windows
and scattered the seeds of sorrow on the threshold

In the evenings, it summons ghosts and memories
The relatives resurrect from old photos
and tell forgotten stories and anecdotes
Their lives take again timid blushes.

It announces to all my friends
- Laughing pumpkins
and cascades of rustling candies
do not match the interior decorations at all.
Don't open the door
to the groups of impish kids.

What For?

Time spilled out of the leaky hourglass
Centuries like sand dunes
flooded across memories.
People forgot about powerful empires.
Ancient gods,
 with cruel hearts and a thirst for blood,
disappeared into the darkness of history.

Little is left to modern times
- only the ruins of buildings and several artifacts.

Ruined stone tablets whisper
about bloody wars and past triumphs,
about the conquests of powerful rulers
and the rulers themselves.
Tears, suffering, wars,
futile sacrifices, death, and pain
-what are they all for?

I pour quartz particles between my fingers
- they fall to the ground
with a soft humming sound.
Gusts of wind spread golden dust.
I realize that
 I am a witness to passing away.
A symbolic gesture
connects the past with the present.

Jackie Davis Allen

Jackie Davis Allen

Jackie Davis Allen, otherwise known as Jacqueline D. Allen or Jackie Allen, grew up in the Cumberland Mountains of Appalachia. As the next eldest daughter of a coal miner father and a stay at home mother, she was the first in her family to attend and graduate from college. Her siblings, in their own right, are accomplished, though she is the only one, to date, that has discovered the gift of writing.

Graduating from Radford University, with a Bachelor's of Science degree in Early Education, she taught in both public and private schools. For over a decade she taught private art classes to children both in her home and at a local Art and Framing Shop where she also sold her original soft sculptured Victorian dolls and original christening gowns.

She resides in northern Virginia with her husband, taking much needed get-aways to their mountain home near the Blue Ridge Mountains, a place that evokes memories of days spent growing up in the Appalachian Mountains.

A lover of hats, she has worn many. Following marriage to her college sweetheart, and as wife, mother, grandmother, teacher, tutor, artist, writer, poet and crafter, she is a lover of art and antiques, surrounding herself, always, with books, seeking to learn more.

In 2015 she authored *Looking for Rainbows, Poetry, Prose and Art*, and in 2017, *Dark Side of the Moon*. Both books of mostly narrative poetry were published by Inner Child Press and were edited by hulya n. yilmaz in 2019, *No Illusions. Through the Looking Glass*, which was nominated to be considered for a Pulitzer Prize by the publisher and editor of Inner Child Press, ltd.

http://www.innerchildpress.com/jackie-davis-allen.php
jackiedavisallen.com

Great-Grandma Lucy

In an age and a place in time, despite
no telephones, distance too far, and the need
to stand out on the porch, to yell
out our impromptu intention,
"She" knew when we'd arrive.

She'd just tell Liza,
her resilient stepdaughter,
"Just put the chicken and dumplings on."

She was Lucy. She had the "sight",
That mysterious insight that comes
from being in tune with the mystery.
Anointed, with the gift of knowing.

The gift of knowing, that comes
from God, to the special ones.
Lucy was blind. She was old, frail.

Lucy was my step-great grandmother.
But I called her Grandma Lucy. .
She with skin translucent, pale,
like the whitest jade, determined
to live life as best as she could.

Aided by my great aunt Liza.
Liza, the care-taker, was the woman
I called "aunt", blissfully unaware
until many decades later, that
she was in fact, my grandpa's sister.

Grandma Lucy was ancient:
To my child's understanding and
Self-doubt as to who she really was,
truth only revealed itself from research.

As from later years' genealogical records.

I held my fears in unsteady check,
while she traced her bony fingers,
across, all over my facial features.
The way of seeing how I'd grown.
It felt strange. Scary. Creepy.

My mother's mother, (my grandmother)
one day, asked me to accompany her
to visit Grandma Lucy, in the hospital.

I resisted. Afraid. Scared. For me,
The hospital held lots of pain, fear.
A place where I'd spent a year.
A place I hoped never to see again.

When told the request was actually
from Grandma Lucy, my self-doubt relented,
I though she might be dying. Oh, no!

I'm glad I went, for later I'd realize,
I had been fulfilling one of Grandma Lucy's
last requests. Soon after, sadly, she passed away,
Her wish come true, to "see" me.
One last time.

And, then the funeral. The cemetery.
Across the road, up the lazy hill.
Above the railroad tracks.
First traversed across a footbridge.
A lazy polluted creek, menacingly dark.
In my ears, a sibling, frightened, hysterical.

Family, relatives, weeping, wailing,
The scene, emotional.

A casket containing Grandma Lucy.
A dark hole, six feet deep.
My sister, hysterical. Beyond control.

Overcome with grief,
with the unknown, so much,
that my parents sent me home.
To care for her. To comfort her.

My grief, set aside, for the time being,
I withheld my tears. So as not to frighten.
Once sister was asleep, they surfaced,
filling up my long dark night.

Worse than a Nightmare

The morning, and I awaken with a start!
It smells like the day after the Fourth of July!
The clang of metal against metal seems
To have run head-on into future's promise.
The sleeping dogs, once silent, agitated,
Are howling. They are barking.
Something tragic has happened.
Someone is desperate, in need of help.
Flames scorch dawn's deep fog.
Unknown are those voices I hear!
Crying, howling, wailing. It is ever
So strange. How did it happen?
How can a child, in her mind's eye, trace
Such a blinded, twisted, tortured path?
The smoke is so heavy, it chokes;
Got to find Momma...Dear God....
Got to find Papa, let him know,
To find Mamma, let her know.
I am not dreaming.
The bloodcurdling screams, God-awful.
Now, they have subsided.
Is it too late for help?
Got to let Mama and Papa know!
Metal against metal sounds, real.
So, too, the squeal of brakes.

Oh, no!
All is silent.
It is ever so quiet.

Stage of Life

Out on the hill, behind the house, in the
Garden soil, my bare feet retrace the path,
To find the patch, where the strawberries grow.

The gooseberries give an illegal show,
Way down below the pink dogwood tree.

Eyes are supposed to shield the truth it knows.
And, of its worth, its sweet taste of visibility,
Its secret remains a recipe within the life.

Of only family names. They hide here,
and there, between the pastry shell.

Sandwiched between the top and bottom.
Merged with strawberries and mulberries,
The gooseberries make a pie.

Like a bird it sings its own song.
Merrily, I sing along.

So happily-long did fleet-feet dance-around
The innocence of days. Hand in hand, strong
voices, brave and nimble, gave truth to youth.

From hands to lips, life was stained and etched:
The essence of the joy of play. And of past days.

And of ways, some remnants remain
As puppets of memory.
The curtain now is drawn.

The play was like in a book of illustrations.
It has closed. It is no more.

The stage, the scenery have faded away...
Does anyone remember those who lived
and played audience to that day's age?

Jackie Davis Allen

Tzemin
Ition
Tsai

Tzemim Ition Tsai

Dr. Tzemin Ition Tsai comes from the Republic of China(Taiwan). In addition to being a professor of literature at a university, he is more committed to writing poems, novels, and proses. He is also an editor of "Reading, Writing and Teaching" academic text, an International editor of "Contemporary dialogues" literary periodical in Macedonia, and Vice-Chairman of the International Jury of the SAHITTO INTERNATIONAL AWARD in Bangladesh, and a columnist for "Chinese Language Monthly" in Taiwan.

In a wide range of literary creations, he is particularly fond of interesting stories or novels, and writing articles or poems about the feelings of nature and human beings. He has won many national literary awards. His literary works have been anthologized and published in books, journals, and newspapers in more than 55 countries and have been translated into more than 24 languages.

The Errant Crossing

Last night, the tide washed away old dreams.
The returning boat upon the water lingers no more.
As mist unveils the path ahead, whose drunken steed lies
forsaken at the crossing?
Along boundless slanting shores, footprints press into the
sand—
This road of years, like the wind, is driven ever forward.
Dust leaves no trace behind—whose vow of fleeting grace?
The lingering hush dissolves into sighs upon the water,
Wearing away all laughter and words.
Twilight descends; the wanderer drifts.
Where lies your rest, within the gentle dream of spring?
Scenery fades in an instant, tides run aground.
You gaze skyward, where distant lights still burn in your
eyes.
This road has no shore.
Wind and rain, heedless, drench resolve.
Farewell to the city's glow; footsteps carve far from what
must not be longed for,
One story after another.
Adrift, one learns to walk alone.
Fate sketches in light strokes—the deepest tale is parting.
Born to the restless path, destined to roam.
Treading dawn and dusk to dust, passing through the ages'
veil.
Boundless expanse—where in this world may time find
rest?
Deep in the soul, a cloud forever unwilling to descend.
Yes, that cloud, still refusing to fall,
Recounts the journey of the errant.

Walking Barefoot Across the Skeleton Of Time

Night, torn asunder by merciless winds.
Moonlight, a page; stars, scattered punctuation.
And we, unfinished sentences,
adrift in the void, searching for syntax.
I walked barefoot across the skeleton of time.
Pebbles, like letters from yesterday,
glimmer with fragments of memory,
too tender to read to the end.
Someone asked,
what lies at the end of the road?
I reached out, pointing to a distant light,
suspended beneath the eaves of darkness for a thousand
millennia,
a tear that refuses to fall.
For a moment, I mistook life
for a tautened string,
awaiting the gentle pluck of time's hand.
I have watched secrets,
tremble into crooked melodies.
Some notes, weightless as wind;
some beats, heavy as stone.
Some choose to breathe between the rests,
some stand still, letting the wind carve their years,
some become drifting sand,
content to slip through time's unclosed fingers.
Like a bird with no homeward sky,
I run through the narrow seams of dusk and dawn,
pressing through crowds, slipping into
the carriage of time,
listening for the wheels of the past to strike
the next perfect rhyme.

Tzemim Ition Tsai

Like an unfinished verse,
I knock with all my might—
but hear only echoes,
finding a star behind the door where the soul may rest.

To Befriend Ink

Sitting by the window, the breeze stirs the slender curtain,
Night deep as ink, the lamp casts a solitary glow.
The desk lies in disarray, pages strewn with unfinished words,
The brush untouched, yet my thoughts soared beyond the eaves.
Beyond the window, the parasol tree whispers low,
Fallen leaves gently tap the stone before the threshold,
Like old friends in quiet vigil, like distant dreams returning.
Far down the alley, scattered lanterns reflect on dampened moss,
Voices recede, leaving only the steady toll of the watch,
stirring the trembling pages.

Beneath the lamp, dark ink as time seeps through,
The hesitant brush trails a path of life's ebb and flow.
Once I wrote of rivers and mountains painted in grandeur,
And once I wrote of hearts sundered by sorrow and joy.
Yet countless tales of the world, when penned to page,
remain but faint traces.
Wax tears fall, like the slow passage of time,
The ink is yet wet, yet uncertain if the morrow shall see its tale complete.
Night dew creeps in, cold fingers brushing my sleeves,
My thoughts roam freely yet always return to this quiet world.

Dawn approaches, the eastern sky faintly pale,
The book is closed, the brush is set beside the inkstone.
The wind stirs once more, carrying away a trace of ink's fragrance,
Leaving behind a stroke yet to dry, awaiting the gaze of future readers.

Tzemim Ition Tsai

Noreen Snyder

Noreen Snyder

Noreen Ann Snyder has been writing since she was a teenager. She writes a variety of different topics. Her favorite poetic forms are Sonnets, Blitz, Haiku, Tanka, and Free Verse. She always learning different poetic forms.

Noreen Ann Snyder is a poet, writer, and an author of five books, (four books are co-authored with her late husband, Garry A. Snyder.) Her poetry is in several Inner Child Press Anthologies. She is the founder ofThe Poetry Club on Facebook.

Break You Or Resilience You

Tragedies will either break you

into depression, anger

or it can make you more resilience,

stronger. It all depends on you.

Look around you- you don't know what

disasters other people are going through.

Show compassion, caring.

Pray for them.

Show others the way!

Help them to be steady, firm

on solid ground.

Grief

Have you experienced grief
that it hit you so hard
when you at least expected it,
tears started to flow freely
then you wept uncontrollably?
At one point in your life,
you'll go through this
once or several times.
Write down your feelings
through a poem, a prose, or
an entry in your journal.
Pray to God-talk to Him-
He will listen to you,
Read a book that you enjoy.
Start a new hobby or two.
Visit with your friends
or make new friends.
Do things in honor of your loved one.
Go ahead and grieve your way
however long it takes.
Grief is NOT brief.
Please don't forget YOU!
Take care of yourself.
You are important!

Spring

I have magical powers
I bring new growth
to the trees and to the flowers.
I bring warmth
to nature.
I give the birds
a reason to sing
and to be happy.
I give the forests
a reason to
feel beautiful.
I have magical powers
for a while. There is hope.
I am Spring.
I'll put a smile
on your face.
I'll make you sing
and be happy.

Elizabeth E. Castillo

Elizabeth Esguerra Castillo

Elizabeth Esguerra Castillo is a multi-awarded and an Internationally-Published Contemporary Author/Poet and a Professional Writer / Creative Writer / Feature Writer / Journalist / Travel Writer from the Philippines. She has 2 published books, "Seasons of Emotions" (UK) and "Inner Reflections of the Muse", (USA). Elizabeth is also a co-author to more than 60 international anthologies in the USA, Canada, UK, Romania, India. She is a Contributing Editor of Inner Child Magazine, USA and an Advisory Board Member of Reflection Magazine, an international literary magazine. She is a member of the American Authors Association (AAA) and PEN International.

Web links:

Facebook Fan Page

https://free.facebook.com/ElizabethEsguerraCastillo

Google Plus

https://plus.google.com/u/0/+ElizabethCastillo

Phoenix Rising

A storm of sorrow, winds of fear,
A tempest's wrath, a bitter tear.
The fragile soul, it bends and sighs,
Beneath the weight of burdened skies.

But deep within, a spark remains,
A flicker bright, dispelling pains.
A quiet strength, a whispered plea,
To rise above, to set us free.

For resilience blooms in darkest night,
A stubborn hope, a guiding light.
From shattered dreams, a new design,
A phoenix rising, pure and fine.

The wounded heart, it learns to mend,
With every trial, it transcends.
Each scar a story, etched in time,
A testament to strength sublime.

The whispered doubt, the chilling dread,
Are overcome, the spirit spread.
A tapestry of pain and grace,
Resilience finds its rightful place.

So let the shadows fall and loom,
For in the depths, a spirit blooms.
A steadfast heart, unyielding will,
Resilience's song, a victory still.

Faith Whispers

A whispered prayer, a hopeful sigh,
A heart ablaze, beneath the sky.
Through trials deep, and storms that roar,
Faith's steadfast flame, forevermore.

A fragile seed, in barren ground,
Can blossom forth, a strength profound.
With roots of hope, and leaves of grace,
A verdant trust, in time and space.

Though shadows fall, and doubts arise,
Faith's guiding light, before our eyes.
A beacon bright, a steady hand,
Across the waves, across the land.

A mountain high, a chasm wide,
Faith's unwavering spirit, inside.
A quiet strength, a heart so true,
Through darkness' grip, it sees it through.

For in the soul, a fire burns,
A sacred trust, where hope returns.
A whispered plea, a fervent prayer,
Faith's gentle touch, banishes despair.

Cloak of Hope

The velvet cloak of night, it slowly yields,
To rosy hues that paint the eastern fields.
A whispered sigh, a gentle, softest breeze,
Stirring the leaves, among the sleeping trees.

The stars, like diamonds, fade and softly gleam,
As golden fingers touch the waking stream.
A painter's brush, across the canvas wide,
With strokes of amber, crimson, and of pride.

The sun ascends, a fiery, golden ball,
Dispelling shadows, answering nature's call.
A symphony of birds, a joyful sound,
As morning's chorus echoes all around.

The dewdrop pearls, upon the grasses bright,
Reflect the glory of the coming light.
A newborn day, with promise, fresh and new,
A canvas painted, vibrant, pure, and true.

From slumber deep, the world awakes anew,
And greets the dawn, with colours fresh and true.
A masterpiece of beauty, born anew,
In every sunrise, ever fresh and true.

Mutawaf Shaheed

Mutawaf Shaheed

C. E. Shy has been writing since the seventh grade. He continued writing through high school, until he became more involved in sports. After his graduation, he worked at the White Motors Company where he wrote for the company's newspaper. He started a column called: "The Poet's Corner." That was his first published work.

www.innerchildpress.com/c-e-shy.php

What Made Ya?

Bending and bowing to that what
made you.
While bending the rules please try not to
break them.

We got some slack on some of that.
I take mercy personal.
There is no such thing
as luck, good or bad.

You can't compare good
and evil to up or down, to black or white,
night and day.
It matters not to me how you handle
your yield.

I'm struggling with mine in
the other field.
Minding my business is the order of the day.
How many twists can you turn? How
many wrongs can you write?

How can you imagine
outside your imagination and come back with an
explanation?
I suggest you start bending and
bowing to that what made you. If you stopped, I
think somebody played you.

Thinking that, that's for me.

Knowing that it couldn't be.
Wishing that it only could.
Knowing that it would do no good.
Crying till my eyes turn pale.

Tears enough for a boat to sail.
With this burden on my heart.
It has driven life and I apart.
But only if I, could physically cry;

If I did, it would be a lie.
My spirit now accepts the fact, as it always does;
It could never be, because it never was.

Mr. Clature

Normen, used to twist words to make them fit.
He was gifted like that. From time to time his
tongue would twist and the words would come
out between
 his teeth.

His way with words was uncanny. He heard
words with his fingers and his lips would lock
around syllables.
He would spit the residue out. Then his mind would go
Clang ,clang. Click.

His thoughts would show up naked. He enjoyed irregular
mind shifts. He watched his pulse on TV. His wife was
named
Norma and she was just common and could hardly wait to
Get away.

hülya
n.
yılmaz

hülya n. yılmaz

Liberal Arts Professor Emerita, hülya n. yılmaz [sic] is Co-Chair and Director of Editing Services at Inner Child Press International, a published author, ghostwriter, and translator (EN, DE, and TU; in any direction). Her literary contributions appeared in a large number of national and international anthologies.

hülya writes creatively to attain and nourish a comprehensive awareness for and development of our humanity.

hülya n. yılmaz, a traveler on the journey called "life" . . .

Writing Web Site
https://hulyanyilmaz.com/

Editing Web Site
https://hulyasfreelancing.com

Grieving

for the complete lack of empathy
toward fellow humans' pain and suffering

grieving
for the swift condemnation
of those who are different on the outside

grieving
for the applauses to cruelty

grieving
for the silence in front of joyful hatred
toward people of diverse colors and socioeconomic classes

grieving
for the dying breath of humanity

what can i

or you can do?

is it not the plan of the powers that be
to make us doubt ourselves?

does *aged* and *physically limited* not
mean to them, "out of order"?

let us not ignore our mental strength
and our resolve to speak for the voiceless

coupled with our compassion for the poor and the weak,
even one single soul's endurance will suffice

hence, the answer to the question,
what can i
or you can do?

a dog in the cemetery

his friend was long dead

for months, he stayed on his grave

loyalty defined

Teresa E. Gallion

Teresa E. Gallion

Teresa E. Gallion is a seeker on a journey to work on unfolding spiritually in this present lifetime. Writing is a spiritual exercise for Teresa. Her passions are traveling the world and hiking the mountain and desert landscapes of the western United States. Her journeys into nature are nurtured by the Sufi poets Rumi and Hafiz. The land is sacred ground and her spiritual temple where she goes for quiet reflection and contemplation. She has published five books: Walking Sacred Ground, Contemplation in the High Desert, Chasing Light, a finalist in the 2013 New Mexico/Arizona Book Awards, Scent of Love, a finalist in the 2021 New Mexico/Arizona Book Awards and Come Egypt in 2024. She has two CDs, *On the Wings of the Wind* and *Poems from Chasing Light*. Her work has appeared in numerous journals and anthologies.

Website: http://teresagallion.yolasite.com/

Harmonic Resilience

Trials and tribulations challenge
our very existence.
We hold our ground on every turn.

With every defeat, we rise again
stronger than before.
A bold fire burns in our veins.

We mend the cracks and start over
steering our perpetual broken wheels.
Resistance is our fight call.

We ride the waves of hope.
Resilience is our guiding light.
We persevere because we can.

Back of Doubt

Whispers from the heart bleed
behind a wall of disbelief.
A broken soul longs to rise,
tired of swimming in low self-esteem.

Weary eyes release a rain of tears
that question self-worth.
A faint voice trembles in fear.
Courage is missing in action.

Follow the light on wings of hope.
Echoes of Spirit sound a warrior's cry.
You must rise-up and touch the sky
to break the back of self-doubt.

Approaching Spring

The world awakens from winter's foothold.
Soft petals slowly spread in mornings light.
Dawn embraces a symphony of hues.

The earth is bloated with rainbow colors
and green sneaks a peek everywhere.
Tender grass sways in the breeze.

The dance of life is reborn in lush beauty.
There is laughter in a stream's gentle flow
while fields of flowers tell fragrant tales.

In gratitude for natures' blessing,
open your arms and embrace
the pure magic of spring.

Ashok K. Bhargava

Ashok K. Bhargava

Ashok Bhargava is a poet, writer, inspirational speaker and a literary consultant. He has attended poetry conferences in Italy, Turkey, India and Philippines. His latest book "Riding the Tide" about his battle with cancer has been translated and published in Arabic, Hindi, Telugu and Bengali languages. He is a contributing writer to several anthologies worldwide including World Poetry Almanac 2014. He has been published in numerous print and online magazines.

Ashok has won many accolades including Poet Ambassador to Japan, Kalidasa International award, World Poetry Lifetime Achievement award, Writers Beyond Borders Peace award and Tapsilog Leadership award for his community involvement. He is founder of Writers International Network Canada Society to discover, nourish, recognize and celebrate writers, poets and artists and to assist them to network with the community at large. He is the author of eight books of poetry and one anthology. He is Artist-in-Residence at Moberly Arts & Cultural Centre and also co-edits the literary section of The Link Newspaper.

Ashok K. Bhargava

Between the Past and the Present

I reacted to your voice, tone and
body language that day

You retorted, doubled down
A toxic fiery clash

Ever since, an icy silence has
withered a blooming garden

To undo what was done
To un-speak what was spoken

Text messages sent
never responded

Apologies to heal
snubbed

Meanings beneath the words
not deciphered

Some days the past comes into the present
simmering

It's painful to see the past and present existing
together in a dreadful knot too stubborn to open

My mind like a crow cawing raucously
hangs onto dry pieces of memories

too hard to nibble, beak clamped
on the cursed bite

Time passes
it does not bring sadness or joy

It's us

Ending Finale
Dedicated to late Lt. General P.D. Bhargava

You were tender yet tough
critical yet caring
feisty yet fair

I can't find words to define you
You were resilient, buoyant,
Spirited, upbeat and determined

You always looked for ways
to help others,
lead the dispirited and those left behind

Where are you now
I like to tell
your absence hurts

I wake up to
morning sky
showering tears

Hues of light
dripping from the bougainvillea
along the fence

It shows me how to bear pain
without sorrow
quietly

Nothing can be done
to bring you back
from mortality

Infinity you are now
a blooming flower
a shining ripple on the river of time

You are within me
immortal
smiling

You Can Never Leave Me

*Poets in ancient China believed, the words stop but the poem goes on
like a canoe, its paddles lifted from the water. (R.G. Evans)*

though　　you　　left　　me
　　　　　　　　　　　　and　　never　　looked　　back

you　　have　　never　　left
　　　　　　　　　　　　my　　heart　　my　　soul

you　　will　　remain　　with　　me
　　　　　　　　　　　　in　　my　　mind　　always

thousand　　codes　　bind
　　　　　　　　　　　　us　　　　together

in　　dreams　　you　　appear
　　　　　　　　　　　　a　　child　　slipping

on　　mossy　　steps
　　　　　　　　　　　　swift　　waters　　of　　Ganges

promising　　me　　later　　to　　scatter
　　　　　　　　　　　　my　　ashes

on　　these　　steps
　　　　　　　　　　　　where　　ancestors　　live

bringing　　tears
　　　　　　　　　　　　in　　my　　eyes

My　　child　　I　　know　　you　　will
　　　　　　　　　　　　return　　to　　me　　someday

Just　　remember　　I
　　　　　　　　　　　　never　　stopped　　loving　　you

Caroline 'Ceri Naz' Nazareno Gabis

Caroline 'Ceri' Nazareno-Gabis

Caroline 'Ceri Naz' Nazareno-Gabis, author of Velvet Passions of Calibrated Quarks, World Poetry Canada International Director to Philippines is a multi-awarded poet, editor, journalist, educator, peace and women's advocate. She believes that learning other's language and culture is a doorway to wisdom.

Among her poetic belts include **Gabrielle Galloni Memorial Panorama International Youth Award 2022,** Panorama Youth Literary Awards 2020, 7th Prize Winner in the 19th, 20th and 21st Italian Award of Literary Festival; Writers International Network-Canada ''Amazing Poet 2015'', The Frang Bardhi Literary Prize 2014 (Albania), Poet Journalist Award 2014 (Tuzla, Istanbul, Turkey) and World Poetry Empowered Poet 2013 (Vancouver, Canada). She's a featured member of Association of Women's Rights and Development (AWID), The Poetry Posse, Galaktika Poetike, Asia Pacific Writers and Translators (APWT), Axlepino and Anacbanua. Her poetry and children's stories have been featured in different anthologies and magazines worldwide.

Links to her works:

http://panitikan.ph/2018/03/30/caroline-nazareno-gabis/

https://apwriters.org/author/ceri_naz/

http://www.aveviajera.org/nacionesunidasdelasletras/id1181.html

Caroline 'Ceri' Nazareno-Gabis

The Wagon of Resilience

When the sun is covered with dark clouds
A storm raged with its mighty hands,
Swept away, the crepuscular rays,
But shadows of the trees, still danced and stood still.

Laughter echoed from the hollow space,
The best medicine you can hold,
Don't be choked with circumstances,
Free yourself from the rumored beasts,
Be the captain of resilience.

Grief Entombed

The whispers grew, a mocking sound

You're weak, lost and barren,

Grief is like a fragile bird with broken wing,

It couldn't fly, it couldn't sing.

Your trembling from a daunting task.

You sighed for a deep cut,

The roots of pain and great loss,

It made one's heart torn and lost.

A Haven of Self -doubt

I watched the rising sun
From the sea of doubts,
I am like a fading wave
That keeps on coming back,
I can feel the tension
From the current,
That fear of not doing,
Incapable of getting the fruits
I am always dreaming of,
But everyday , I look upon
The weeds growing,
In between the jagged rocks and cracked soil,
It gives me a hopeful hue,
A green, fresh chance,
To live and trust myself

Swapna Behera

Swapna Behera is a trilingual poet, translator, environmentalist, editor from India and author of seven books of different genres including one on children's literature on Environment. She is the recipient of International UGADI AWARD 2019, honoured from Gujurat Sahitya Akademi 2022, 2021 International Poesis Award of Honor as Jury, Pentasi B World Fellow Poet, Honoured Poet of India from Seychelles Government and International awards from Algeria, Morocco, Kajhakhstan, modern Arabic Literary Renaissance of Egypt, International Arts Council Argentina etc. Her stories, poems, articles are published in many International and National magazines and ezines. Her poem A NIGHT IN THE REFUGEE CAMP is translated into 67 languages. She has received over 60 National and International Awards. At present she is the Cultural Ambassador for India and South Asia of Inner Child and the life member of Odisha Environmental Society

Email
swapna.behera@gmail.com

Web Site
http://swapnabehera.in/

autobiography of a moon

I am the moon in your courtyard
a patch of green peace
covering the cynical silhouette
or the satanic scowls
I am the eternal child
dancing on the lush green pasture
my self-identity in tandem with geraniums
the carcasses of my skin, blood or bone
will recreate a new calendar
love weaves and creates
I have borrowed couplets from cuckoo and peacock
I will build my own roof
I can construct my road on the sanitary napkins
my femininity will hoist the flags of my verbs
I am a noun, a dot, a river
a declaration of virgin dreams on the green valley
who can delete me?
I am a journey

A poet is dying tonight

a poet is dying tonight;
In a panacea of blood
Enough of transfusion, transmission
and lots of confusion
he **is** in love with the widow droplets on the grass
Love is a forbidden Adam's apple
a poet is not a **pet** or the slave of the society
His heart is on lease
He can neither smile or cry
Has to be in the syndrome of hangover
A poet is dying tonight
Tired and sleepless,
wrapping the blankets of the stars
The tattoo of time on his soul
Is he the broken bangle pieces
to celebrate peace?
Or a prism to refract the beam of light?
a stamped flesh hung in the butcher's shop?
A poet is dying tonight; before comes the twilight
The world is ready for the funeral condolences
Let him die peacefully
For thousands are in the queue
To be the martyrs, to be the poets 1

metamorphosis of a midnight deal

December midnight

A deal for a blanket

In the footpath

To save the frozen blood

Just a midnight deal

the red signature

of the document

on her torn frock

Simply a deal

in the dark subway

For a blanket!!!

 why at all?

Albert 'Infinite' Carrasco

Albert 'Infinite' Carassco

Albert "Infinite The Poet" Carrasco is an urban poet, mentor and public speaker.

Albert believes his experience of growing up in poverty, dealing with drugs and witnessing murder over and over were lessons learnt, in order to gain knowledge to teach. Albert's harsh reality and honesty is a powerfully packed punch delivered through rhyme. Infinite grew up in the east part of the Bronx and still resides there, so he knows many young men will follow the same dark path he followed looking for change. The life of crime should never be an option to being poor but it is, very often.

Infinite poetry @lulu.com

Alcarrasco2 on YouTube

Infinite the poet on reverbnation

Infinite Poetry

www.lulu.com/us/en/shop/al-infinite-carrasco/infinite-poetry/paperback/product-21040240.html

www.innerchildpress.com/albert-carrasco

Resilience, Grief, Self-Doubt

Being able to dream with hope is my "super power". If I dreamt it I could live it, I figured if it's my calling I must answer. I don't care if there was roaches in my cereal box, or the fact that the household had to be silent after hearing that loud obnoxious, your rent is months late NYCHA knock, I didn't care if the fridge and cabinets were bare. I'm my dreams my family and I lived wealthy and healthy, regardless to the fact that at the present time, that wasn't our reality. Settling for less wasn't me, the past couldn't affect my future, I endured many trials and tribulations but wasn't going to drown in my woes, my resilience not to stay down set my mind free. Grief is a big part of who I am. I mean since I was a kid I've been grief stricken, when my father died I was only twelve years old, that's when the grief kicked in and through the years I've dealt with back to back deaths, grief kept on kick'n. Hurt, pain and poverty's oppression causes stagnation, but no matter what was my situation, if I was stuck between a rock and a hard place, hope was my lubrication. Self doubt was never a ball and chain, I always knew that one day hope will be my umbrella to somber rain. It did. people on different continents know my name because they read my work and feel my pain. The little boy that grew up in the projects is considered by many to be like an urban prophet

Kimberly Burnham

Kimberly Burnham

A brain health expert (PhD in Integrative Medicine) and award-winning poet, Kimberly Burnham lives with her wife and family in Spokane, Washington. Kim speaks extensively on peace, brain health, and *"Awakenings: Peace Dictionary, Language and the Mind, a Daily Brain Health Program."* She recently published *"Heschel and King Marching to Montgomery A Jewish Guide to Judeo-Tamarian Imagery."* Currently work includes *"Call and Response To Maya Stein an Anthology of Wild Writing"* and a how-to non-fiction book, *"Using Ekphrastic Fiction Writing and Poetry to Create Interest and Promote Artists, Writers, and Poets."*

Follow her at https://amzn.to/4fcWnRB

Because I Am Resilient

I am resilient because

I have lived in five countries on four continents
I know how to adapt, to move, to listen
to express curiosity and admiration
to learn from others

I have studied many cultures and religious traditions
I can appreciate the similarities and differences
guava paste, Belgian chocolate, sushi, veggie burgers, and
humus
I am better for believing in something greater than myself

I have molded my brain with several languages
entered new worlds through books
created from the cultures, traditions, and minds of others
I write what is in my heart and mind
and listen to those around me

I can forgive
I understand what it is to hurt another
and how even though I didn't set out to anger and sadness
I am human and know both empathy and regret

I can love deeply like a river
each day renewing feelings and desires
thinking of myself and another's needs
I feel and act on tenderness and joy

Because I am resilient
I can live, learn, act, forgive and love

Where is God

I once had a conversation or really a series of conversations
with a friend who doesn't believe
in god

What I came to is I have no idea if god exists
but in a boundless universe I can allow
for a being greater than myself

I am better for believing in something greater
not better than another but a better version of myself
I can, of course, hold my-self accountable
somehow it seems easier accompanied by
the thought of someone watching over me

Like the Jewish mothers who used to go each day
standing by the gates between Gaza and Israel
giving Israeli soldiers a reminder
someone like their own mothers watching
how they treat others

Now there is no one crossing
the gates all barricaded
bombs flying back and forth across the walls
and I wonder where god is
that something greater than myself

If there is no one or nothing greater
what now is my responsibility
if I choose sides
what does that make me
in this world with so much great
and hate

Self-Doubt

I get nervous at work because people expect miracles
and I can't even get close
I do know how to feel anatomy and physiology
the rhythms and flows of a human form
to talk to people and help them notice the good that is
happening
maybe I am highlighting the placebo effect
but even though I don't always know what I am doing
the placebo effect is not nothing

I know how to listen with my ears and heart and hands
in time listening can solve a lot of problems
if I wait long enough and listen hard enough
life and the body changes despite not knowing
all that I am doing

Sometimes when I have my hands on a person and get
distracted
what I am trying to do happens because I am not in the way
leaving the me that knows all that I need to know
and already does what is needed
a little pressure here to remind the body how to heal
because that's what bodies want—to heal

My imposter syndrome kicks up when something good
happens
but I am not making claims or promises
still it scares me that everyone will realize
I don't know what I am doing and they will be disappointed
or angry that I have misrepresented myself but I haven't
I have only stood by as others do
but if I talk about my feelings my inadequacies

the placebo effect which is not nothing maybe lost
and so I respond, I listen, I treat and try but mostly I get out
of my own way
so the part that is doing something good
can continue even when there is a part that doesn't know

Eliza
Segiet

Eliza Segiet

Eliza Segiet graduated with a Master's Degree in Philosophy at Jagiellonian University.

Received *Global Literature Guardian Award* – from Motivational Strips, World Nations Writers Union and Union Hispanomundial De Escritores (UHE) 2018.

Nominated for the Pushcart Prize 2019, 2021.

Laureate *Naji Naaman Literary Prize 2020*,

International Award Paragon of Hope (2020),

World Award 2020 *Cesar Vallejo* for Literary Excellence. Laureate of the Special Jury *Sahitto International Award* 2021, World Award *Premiul Fănuş Neagu* 2021.

Finalist *Golden Aster Book* World Literary Prize 2020, *Mili Dueli* 2022, Voci nel deserto 2022.

At the international Festival of Poetry CAMPIONATO MONDIALE DI POESIA (2021/2022) she won the title of vice-champion of the world.

Award BHARAT RATNA RABINDRANATH TAGORE INTERNATIONAL AWARD (2022).

Award - *World Poets Association* (2023).

Laureate Between words and infinity *"International Literary Award (2023).*

The Quivers of Life

What to do when
from tiny seeds
emerge roots
that offer no relief?
When life's adversities
surround us
like grains of a Saharan desert
in a sandstorm?
We must act!
Seek a way!
How to slowly
remove from ourselves bad quivers of life,
this torrent of gales?
Some seek the path of survival in God.
In the hope that prayer will soothe them
– they move in that direction,
while others continue to search.
Will they find it?
The most important thing is to be aware
that nothing lasts forever –
that can bring relief.

Translated by Dorota Stępińska

Cataclysm

He thought
that his world full of smiles
would last forever.
He was wrong!
He always wanted more
than he himself could achieve.
When the two worlds met:
one of possibility, the other of its absence,
it turned out
that between them lay a deep chasm
from which he might
never be able to emerge.
Before, his driving force was Her –
his Mother.
She is gone. She is no more!
He whispered to himself:
Without her, I can't do it! I can't!
We are forever disconnected.
There are no words
that would describe such a loss.
Sadness, despair, regret…
It feels like some bad joke.
Cataclysm –
this best illustrates a family
trying to rebuild a home from the ashes.

Translated by Dorota Stępińska

Triumph

All she could do was to admire
the successes of others.
She herself
didn't have the courage
to try and be good
at piloting,
windsurfing,
or anything else.
She convinced herself
that she couldn't!
She didn't even try
to add wind to her dreams,
to reach another, unknown place,
whose name was –
triumph.
To fight for oneself is more than
to surrender.
To fight for oneself is more than
to exist with the belief of *I can't*.

Translated by Dorota Stępińska

William S. Peters Sr.

Bill's writing career spans a period of well over 50 years. Being first Published in 1972, Bill has since went on to Author in excess of 50+ additional Volumes of Poetry, Short Stories, etc., expressing his thoughts on matters of the Heart, Spirit, Consciousness and Humanity. His primary focus is that of Love, Peace and Understanding!

Bill says . . .

I have always likened Life to that of a Garden. So, for me, Life is simply about the Seeds we Sow and Nourish. All things we "Think and Do", will "Be" Cause and eventually manifest itself to being an "Effect" within our own personal "Existences" and "Experiences" . . . whether it be Fruit, Flowers, Weeds or Barren Landscapes! Bill highly regards the Fruits of his Labor and wishes that everyone would thus go on to plant "Lovely" Seeds on "Good Ground" in their own Gardens of Life!

to connect with Bill, he is all things Inner Child

www.iaminnerchild.com

Personal Web Site

www.iamjustbill.com

Resilience ~ Grief ~ Self Doubt

Beyond my grief
For the loss of my loved one
Lying in wait for me
In the horizons of my heart
Waiting to ambush me
Was a self-induced doubt
That I could ever be loved again
As I had before

As I forced my self
To push forward
Regardless the circumstance
I had an epiphany
And I realized
That there was a certain resilience
I possessed
And my fortitude and courage
Blossomed

just a write a right

my pen wants to come out to play
what do you say
can i frolic in your garden
where consciousness visits
sometimes

my rhymes are amiss
and i tell you this
i don't give a flying whatever
about that endeavor

i am more about
how clever
my delivery may be
and what subverted messages
i can allow you to see
you see
i don't
so won't you take this
meandering journey with me
and perhaps
we can discover
uncover
something wonderful

there are profane
words
from inane mind
reminding me
of the insanity
i embrace

not often
am i so willing

to face my self
or have to taste my self
and my shit

most times
as the prosecutor, judge and jury
i acquit my self
no worry
i will be redeemed

and to those esteemed ones
like he who peers at me
in that mirror
leering at me
jeering and jibing
while i am scribing . .
go take another nap
i will call you when i am done
poking fun at us
trust me
or not
but yesterday i forgot
something
and a happy face "LOL" and hearts to you
boo
love you too

funny what one may get
when they allow
let
their pens come out to play

today ?
did we have anything significant to say
perhaps another nay

or an aye
but know this
i wrote anyway
what did you do ?

just a write a right

Alchemist

With just a little hope,

And some well positioned dreams,

A bucket full of will,

And a heart full of humanity,

And we can change the world!

April
2025
Featured Poets

~ * ~

Gopal Sinha

Taghrid Bou Merhi

Irma Kurti

Marlon Salem Gruezo

I FLY
because
I Can
. . . said the Dreamer to the world.

www.iamjustbill.com

Gopal Sinha

Gopal Sinha

Gopal Sinha is a Civil Engineering graduate, retired government servant, now devotes his time in reading, writing, singing old Hindi film songs, occasionally drawing, photography and of course spending his time with family and friends.

He writes poems, short stories, short essays, reports etc, regularly, in Hindi and English and his articles have been part of many magazines, journals and anthologies, also takes part in on-line poetry recitations and anchoring such a programme.

A request to rain

Pitter patter rain drops,
Clouds seen hill atop,
Little, fine drops of water,
Pouring down like gentle shower,
Bringing hope on farmers' face
Children coming out in open space,
To take the shower, enjoy the first rain,
Elders trying to admonish in vain,
Would shout, run, play, slip, strain,
In the mud, without feeling so much pain,
Lovers, poets, artists having a day,
Some tender feelings, desires,
Emotions, creations on the way,
Good news for the waiting crops,
May I request you,
Before a deluge, please stop.

Unknown paths

It is an unknown path,
Yet, I have ventured out,
Enthusiasm is my guide,
Curiosity, I can't hide.

Slowly I started slowly, moved gently,
Taking steps further cautiously,
Exploring the route with open eyes,
Has been my choice obviously.

Have come across some beautiful sights,
Shady trees, bushes, flowers bright,
Sharp bends, ditches, steep slopes,
Can give you a plausible fright.

Road not always running straight,
Up and down, sometimes flat,
Scattered potholes and many curves,
Being patient, have to keep my nerves.

Where is it leading to,
What comes next,
Though I am not sure,
I make uncertainty, no pretext.

It is easier to choose a path beaten,
I have willingly chosen one untrodden.

Wilted flowers

Once they adorned the garden,

Such is the phase of time,
They have now become a burden !

The flowe-tree that used to be,
The main attraction,
Its branches heavily laden,
With beautiful flowers,
Colourful, smiling, scented,
Showing majestic demeanor, power,
Now stand wilted, a bit neglected.

Counting their days,
Remembering their past,
When they used to get
Everyone's love, care and praise,
Now, as if an outcast !

So is the life,
It happens with everyone,
By taking a lesson,
Be like a flower, not a thorn,
Live your life full,
Seeking a purpose,
Makes it more meaningful.

Taghrid Bou Merhi

Taghrid Bou Merhi

She is a multilingual Lebanese-Brazilian poet, writer, author, essayist, editor, journalist and translator. She has authored 23 books and translated 43 books to date, 112 article to date. She is an active member of various literary and creative platforms. Her writings are part of several national and international magazines, newspapers, journals and anthologies. She is the President of the Camara International of Writers and Artists (Lebanon) and she was chosen among the top 20 international journalist's from Legacy Crown. She is a global advisor for poetry on CCTV Chinese TV and editor and head of the translation department at various literary newspapers and magazine. She has won many awards for her write-ups.

Alphabet of the Soul

Words, like the wind,
move through silence,
carrying secrets within
that only souls can unveil.
They are the space that expands for dreams
and shrinks at the borders of reality.
They speak the unseen,
breaking the silence of lost times.

Words are light spilling
into the darkness of minds,
building bridges of hope
on the shores of defeat.
At times, they are a gentle melody
singing to pain,
and at times, a scream exploding
into a strange horizon.

They are the letters we utter,
yet they dwell within us,
born in our depths,
growing like trees in silence.
They pulse in the heart of time,
traveling with the winds
to reshape the face of destiny.

Words are birds
seeking a homeland in the sky,
singing to the distant,
carrying sorrow like a tear
in the eyes of the stars.

They are the promises we exchange,
yet sometimes, they melt
like wax in the fires of reality.
And despite everything,
they remain a hope floating
on the surface of a deep sea.

The Tattoo of Water

The sea's waters carve their tattoo into my skin with every tide,
And my artery coils around the meaning shattered at the shore—this moment—

My left heart beats to the rhythm of jazz rising from a distant balcony,
While your right heart trembles beneath the feet of crowds chanting for freedom in the alleys.
How do our pulses meet upon the same wave?
Between them, an ocean wrestles with a memory perforated by longing and fractured uproar.

The sea's waters vanish into the sand's thirst without a sound,
Its waves bow like untitled poems,
And seagulls watch your fingers as they reshape the horizon,
Yet the final word drowned in the foam of silence.

I wanted to write a text unscarred by loss,
But the salt seeped into my wound to the bone,
And words overflowed from me like a wave,
Then faded—
Into the sea's toxic silence forever...

MUSIC!

Art adds brilliance to simplicity and illuminates a bright
and elegant dawn.
The most beautiful arts are in harmony with music; in it, I
see a bright and beautiful day.
Nature has unleashed its melodies, the perfect harmonies of
the natural world.
Flowers bloom to the sound of love, spreading an emotion
of loyalty.
Roses listen to beauty and rejoice, flowers in embroidered
attire are leaves.
And on the branches of banana trees, singers chant a
melody of longing for reunion.
The melody of the lute has become a balm for my soul, and
my heart has risen and soared.
And when the nightingales excelled and shone, the melody
of love radiated in this existence.
The melody of the violin inspires me, and I remain
immersed in the language of harmony.
The flute and the oboe are instruments of joy; you are the
sigh of the flower when it blooms.
The melodies unite in Sika or Seba
And the hymns of Rast and Nahound are heard softly in the
hearts.

Taghrid Bou Merhi

Irma
Kurti

Irma Kurti is an Albanian poet, writer, lyricist, journalist, and translator and has been writing since she was a child. She is a naturalized Italian and lives in Bergamo, Italy. Kurti has won numerous literary prizes and awards in Albania, Italy, Switzerland, USA, Philippines, Lebanon and China. Irma Kurti has published 28 books in Albanian, 24 in Italian, 15 in English, and two in French. She has also translated 19 books by different authors, and all of her own books into Italian and English. Her books have been translated and published in 15 countries.

Disorientated

Early morning.
My thoughts
wander,
disorientated,
without
knowing yet
what direction
to take.

The sun road
that radiates
colors, light
full of magic
or the alley
of a gray cloud?

Early morning.
Only the echo
of my thoughts
is heard as they
crash with one
another and
rotate as in a
game, trying
to choose
between sun
and shade.

Ice Between My Fingers

I wanted to hear your voice.
My heart would blossom like
a flower; my joy would flow
just like a stream through the
long telephone wire.

I would bring the spring into
my hands, bird songs, a wealth
of buds. I would watch this
scary and chaotic world with
happy and loving eyes.

I wanted to hear your voice
and touch happiness with
my hands, but they feel cold,
so between my fingers
I now have only ice and frost.

We Had The Sea Close By

We had the sea close by; wide and infinite
in its anger, it tried hard to enter our words.
We had the sea close by; it didn't take much
to hold the waves in our hands. Only a step
would be enough, and the particles of sand
between our fingers would have penetrated.

But I had you close to my soul. The noises,
the waves vanished at sunset, a thousand
particles of sand faded, lost somewhere. It
was your voice that remained; like a cradle
it rocked me with the tenderness of a wave.

Marlon Salem Gruezo

Marlon Salem Gruezo

Marlon Salem Gruezo is a Filipino-Spanish peace and culture advocate, and arts & letters protagonist, and a member of some notable international non-government organisations whose core missions are peace, culture, arts and education promotions. A poetry enthusiast, writer and editor of several international online and print magazines. He was born on March 11, 1973 in Santa Cruz Laguna Philippines. Some of his poems were published in some of the most respected online literary platforms and leading international newspapers and included in poetry anthology books.

Poem of Peace

In a world where hearts can heal,
Where love and understanding seal,
Let us mend our broken seams,
Creating peace from hopeful dreams.

With open hearts and open minds,
Embrace the bonds that truly bind,
Respect and kindness, side by side,
Together, strong, our hopes reside.

No walls to build, no lines to trace,
In every soul, a common grace,
To love, to cherish, and to share,
A world where everyone can care.

So let us tread this path so bright,
With peace as our guiding light,
In unity, our voices blend,
A world of love, on which we depend.

Through storm and strife, we stand as one,
With courage bright as morning sun,
In every heart, a spark to ignite,
A flame of peace, shining so bright.

Let kindness flow from hand to hand,
Across the seas, throughout the land,
Together, we shall make a start,
To build a world where peace resides in every heart.

In the Heart of the Storm

When shadows fall and nights stretch on,
And every step feels weak and wrong,
A whisper stirs, a gentle song,
Hope's tender light, steadfast and strong.

In darkest hours, when tears draw near,
And hearts are clenched by silent fear,
A spark ignites, a flame so clear,
Hope's warm embrace, forever dear.

Through trials faced and battles fought,
When dreams seem lost, and courage caught,
A beacon shines, with love it's wrought,
Hope's guiding star, a cherished thought.

When life is harsh, and paths are steep,
And weary souls long for sleep,
A promise blooms, in hearts to keep,
Hope's gentle hand, a vow so deep.

So hold on tight, through storm and strife,
For in the pain, there's still new life,
A dawn will break, an end to strife,
Hope's endless song, renews our life.

My Christmas Wish

In the glow of twinkling lights so bright,
Snowflakes dance through the silent night.
Your laughter, a melody, pure and true,
Never did I dream I'd feel this way about you.

Beneath the mistletoe, our hearts entwine,
Whispers of love, like aged wine.
Your touch, a warmth that melts the frost,
In your embrace, I find what was lost.

The scent of pine, the crackling fire,
Each moment with you stokes my desire.
Gifts wrapped in ribbons, but none compare,
To the gift of you, beyond all compare.

Stars above in a velvet sky,
Reflect the sparkle in your eye.
With every carol, my heart sings too,
Never did I dream I'd feel this way about you.

As the world is wrapped in winter's grace,
I find my home in your embrace.
This Christmas, my love, my wish is clear,
To hold you close, year after year.

Remembering

our fallen soldiers of verse

Janet Perkins Caldwell

February 14, 1959 ~ September 20, 2016

Alan W. Jankowski

16 March 1961 ~ 10 March 2017

Shareef Abdur Rasheed

30 May 1945 ~ 11 February 2025

The Butterfly Effect

"IS" in effect

Inner Child Press

News

Published Books

by

Poetry Posse Members

We are so excited to share and announce a few of the current books, as well as the new and upcoming books of some of our Poetry Posse authors.

On the following pages we present to you ...

Alicja Maria Kuberska

Jackie Davis Allen

Gail Weston Shazor

hülya n. yılmaz

Nizar Sartawi

Elizabeth E. Castillo

Faleeha Hassan

Fahredin Shehu

Kimberly Burnham

Caroline 'Ceri' Nazareno

Eliza Segiet

Teresa E. Gallion

Mutawaf Shaheed

William S. Peters, Sr.

Now Available

www.innerchildpress.com

KREW ŻYCIA

The Blood of Life

Eliza Segiet

Translated by Dorota Stępińska

Now Available
www.innerchildpress.com

Now Available

www.innerchildpress.com

Bir Zamanlar

Türkiye'de

hülya n. yılmaz

Now Available
www.innerchildpress.com

I Am in Your Head

C. E. Shy

Now Available
www.innerchildpress.com

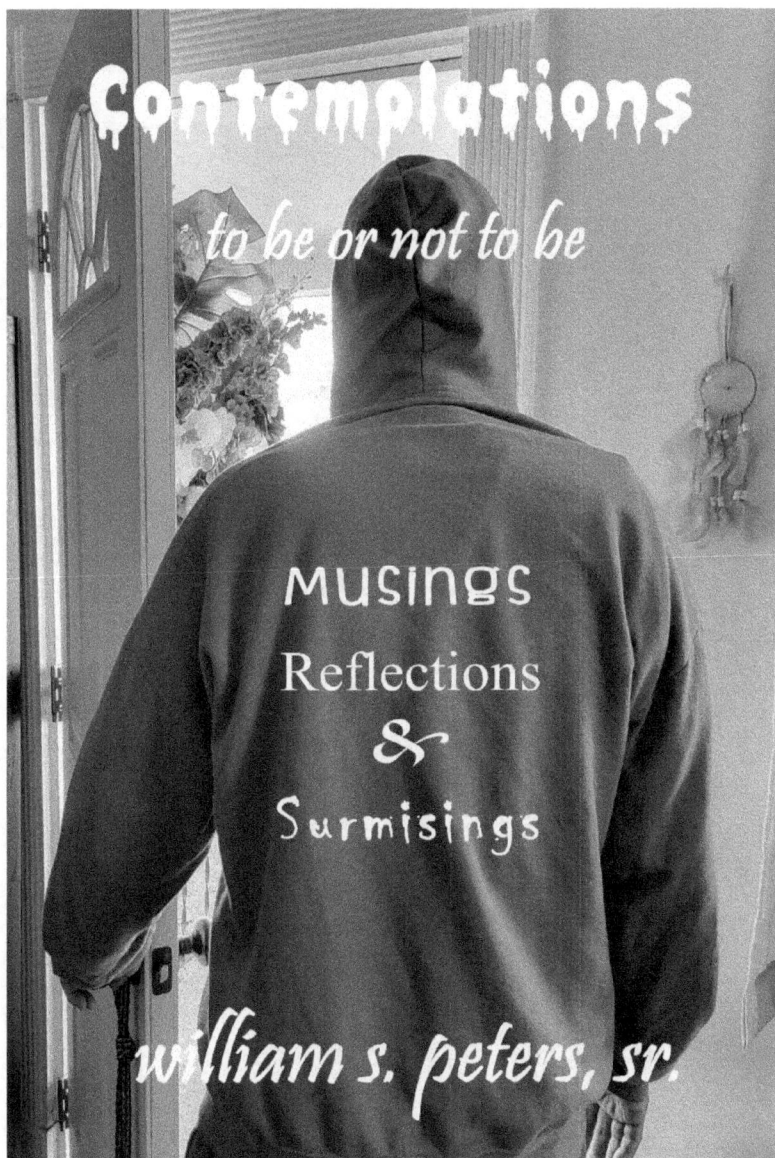

Contemplations

to be or not to be

Musings
Reflections
&
Surmisings

william s. peters, sr.

Now Available
www.innerchildpress.com

Come Egypt

Poetry by

Teresa E. Gallion

Now Available

www.innerchildpress.com

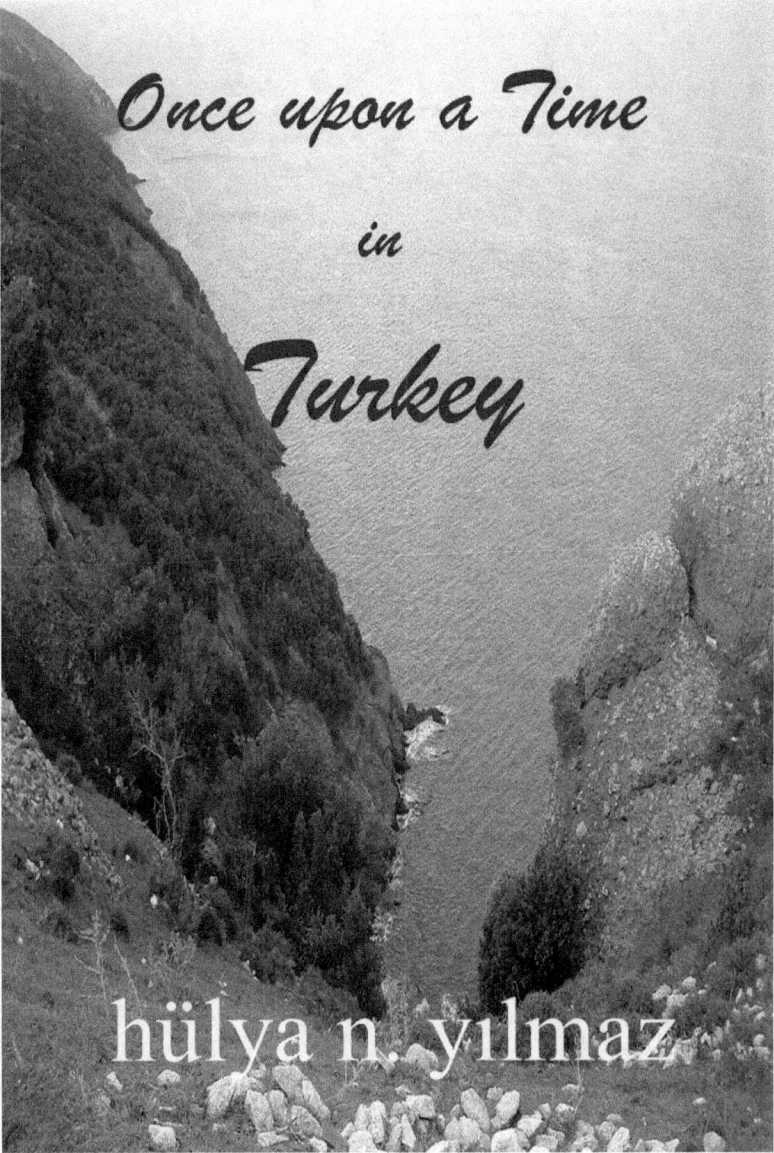

Once upon a Time

in

Turkey

hülya n. yılmaz

Now Available
www.innerchildpress.com

Unapologetically

BLACK

&

Blues

william s. peters, sr.

Now Available
www.innerchildpress.com

Pulling Coats

Shareef Abdur-Rasheed

Now Available
www.innerchildpress.com

UMAMI

The Essence of Deliciousness

Fahredin Shehu

Now Available

www.innerchildpress.com

After the Frost

Alicja Maria Kuberska

Now Available

www.innerchildpress.com

Fahredin Shehu

O R M U S

Now Available

www.innerchildpress.com

Ahead of My Time

. . . from the Streets to the Stages

Albert *Infinite* Carrasco

Now Available
www.innerchildpress.com

Eliza Segiet

To Be More

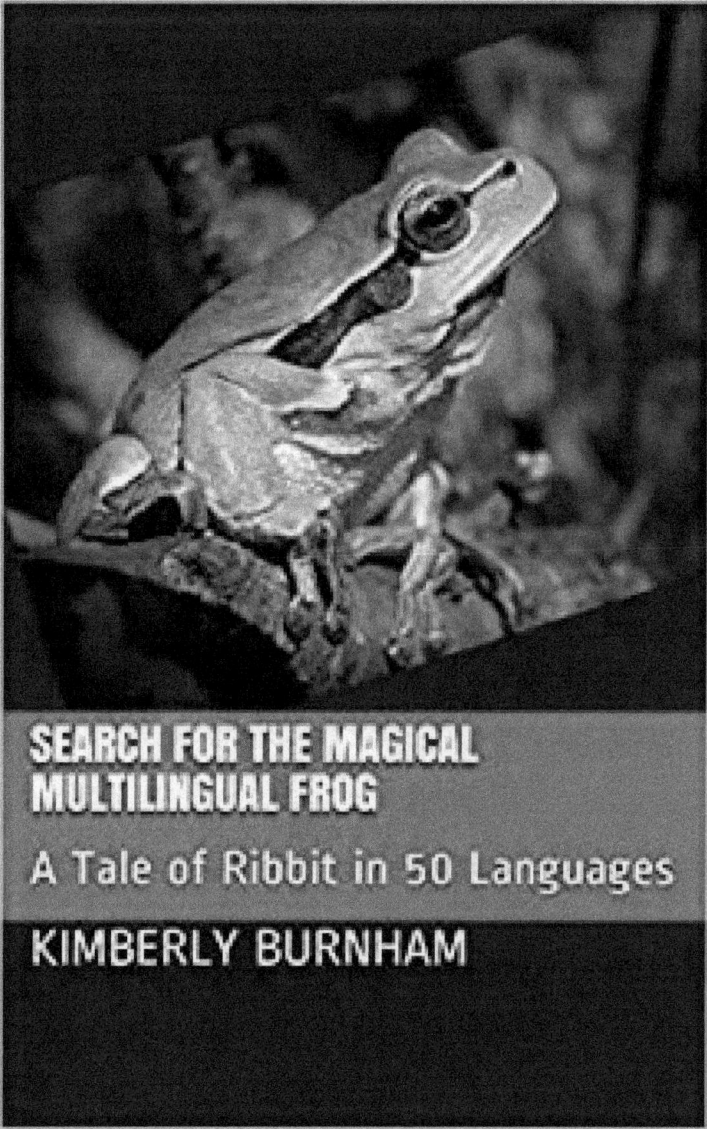

SEARCH FOR THE MAGICAL MULTILINGUAL FROG

A Tale of Ribbit in 50 Languages

KIMBERLY BURNHAM

Now Available at

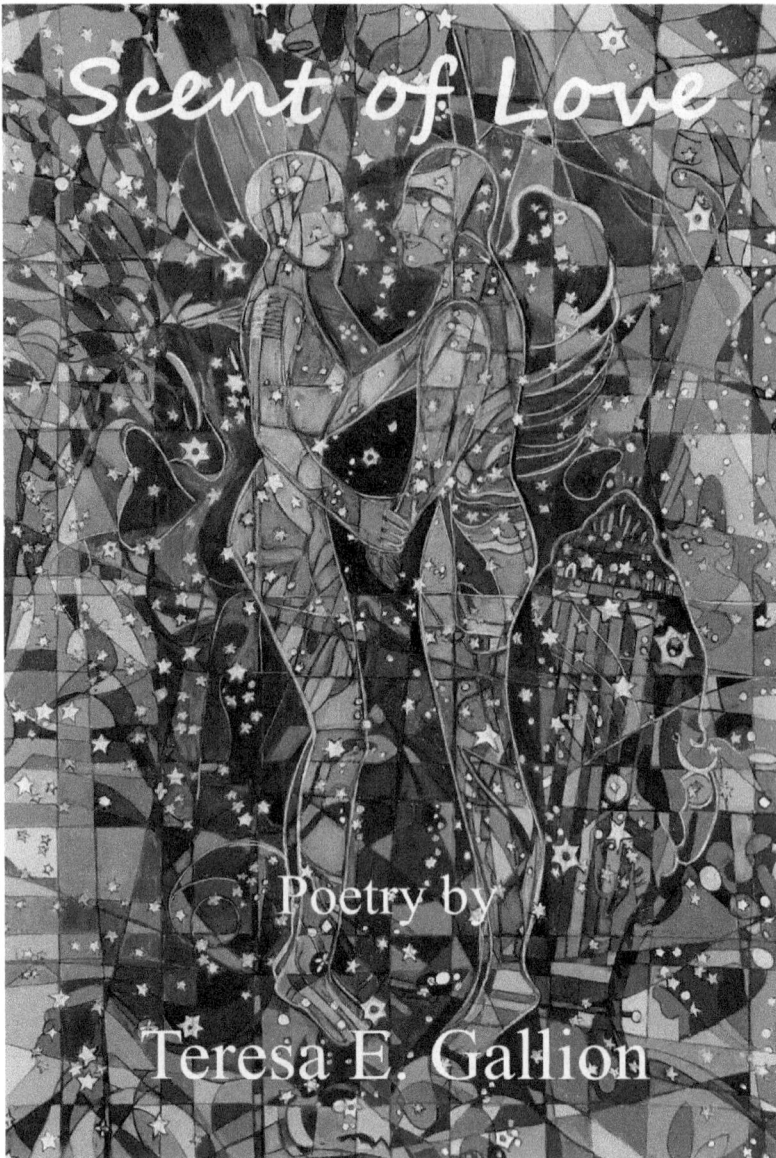

Scent of Love

Poetry by

Teresa E. Gallion

Now Available
www.innerchildpress.com

Inner Reflections
of the
Muse

Elizabeth Castillo

Now Available
www.innerchildpress.com

Letter - Poems

from a Beloved

hülya n. yılmaz

Now Available
www.innerchildpress.com

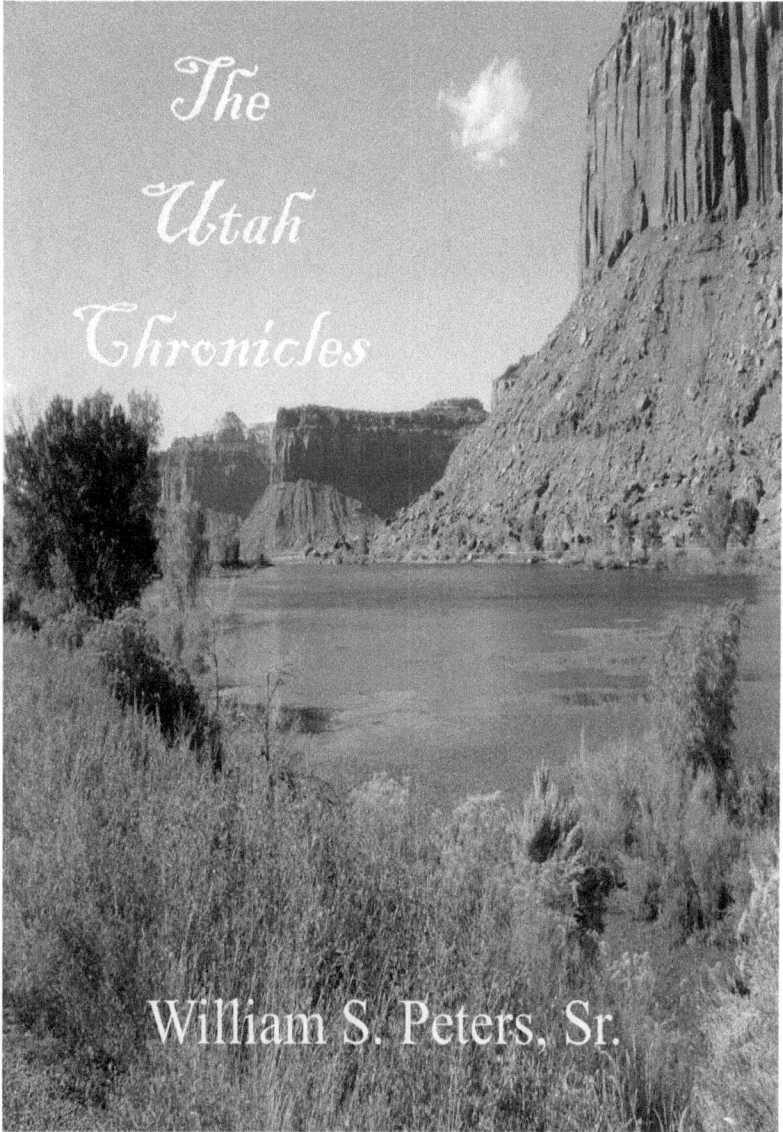

The
Utah
Chronicles

William S. Peters, Sr.

Now Available
www.innerchildpress.com

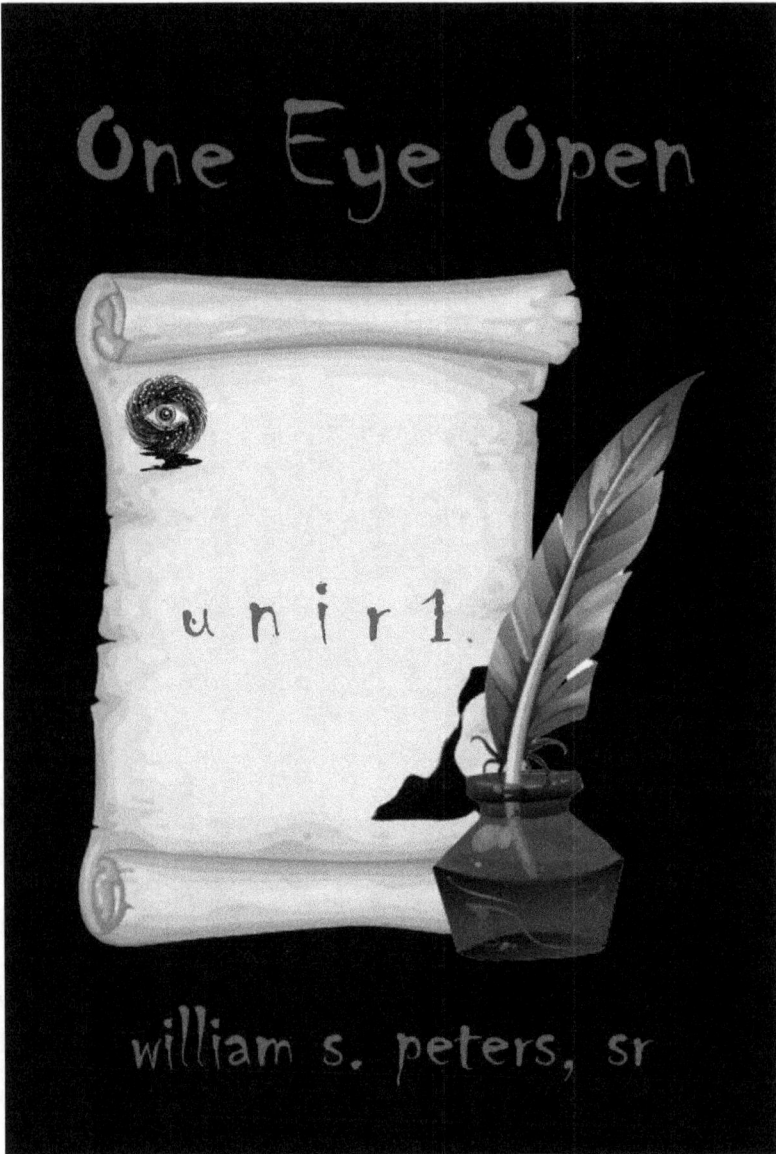

One Eye Open

u n i r 1.

william s. peters, sr

Now Available
www.innerchildpress.com

The Book of krisar

volume v

william s. peters, sr.

Now Available

www.innerchildpress.com

The Book of krisar

Volume I

william s. peters, sr.

The Book of krisar

Volume II

william s. peters, sr.

Now Available

www.innerchildpress.com

The Book of krisar

Volume III

william s. peters, sr.

The Book of krisar

Volume IV

william s. peters, sr.

Now Available

www.innerchildpress.com

*V*elvet *P*assions

of

Calibrated Quarks

Caroline Nazareno-Gabis

Now Available

www.innerchildpress.com

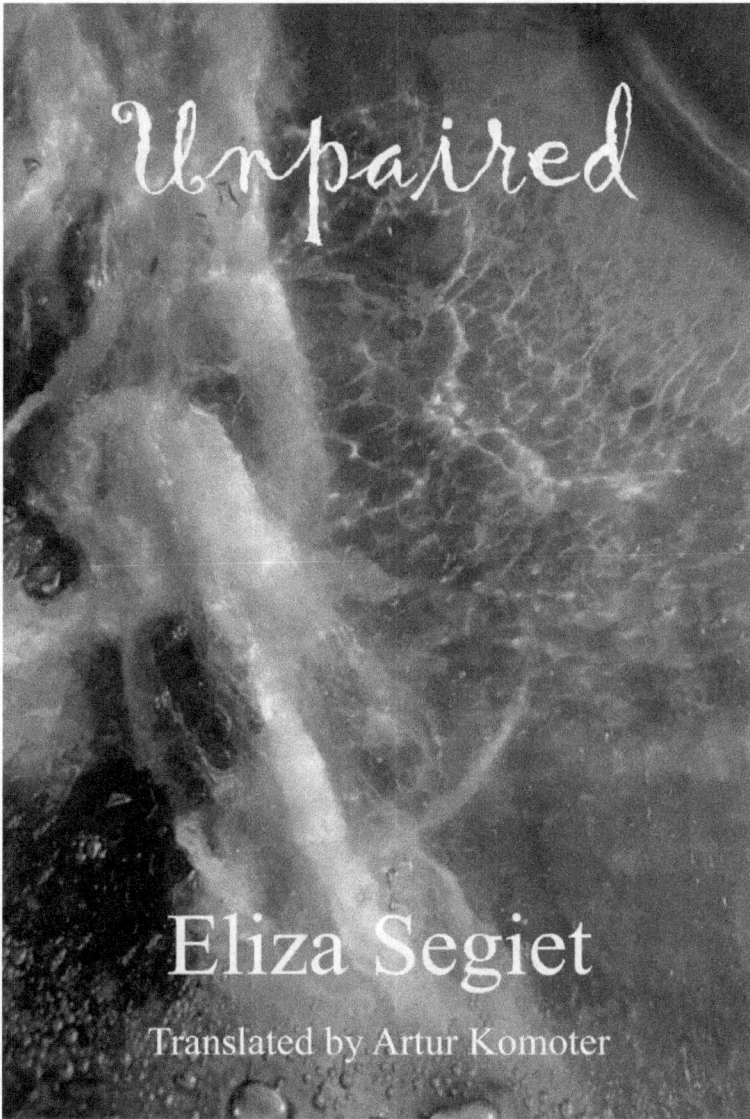

Unpaired

Eliza Segiet

Translated by Artur Komoter

Now Available
www.innerchildpress.com

Canlarım

My Lifeblood

poetry in Turkish and English

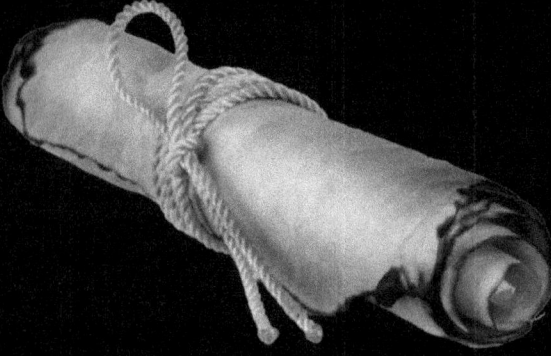

hülya n. yılmaz

Private Issue

www.innerchildpress.com

Butterfly's Voice

Faleeha Hassan

Translated by William M. Hutchins

Now Available at
www.innerchildpress.com

No Illusions

Through the Looking Glass

Jackie Davis Allen

Now Available at
www.innerchildpress.com

Now Available at
www.innerchildpress.com

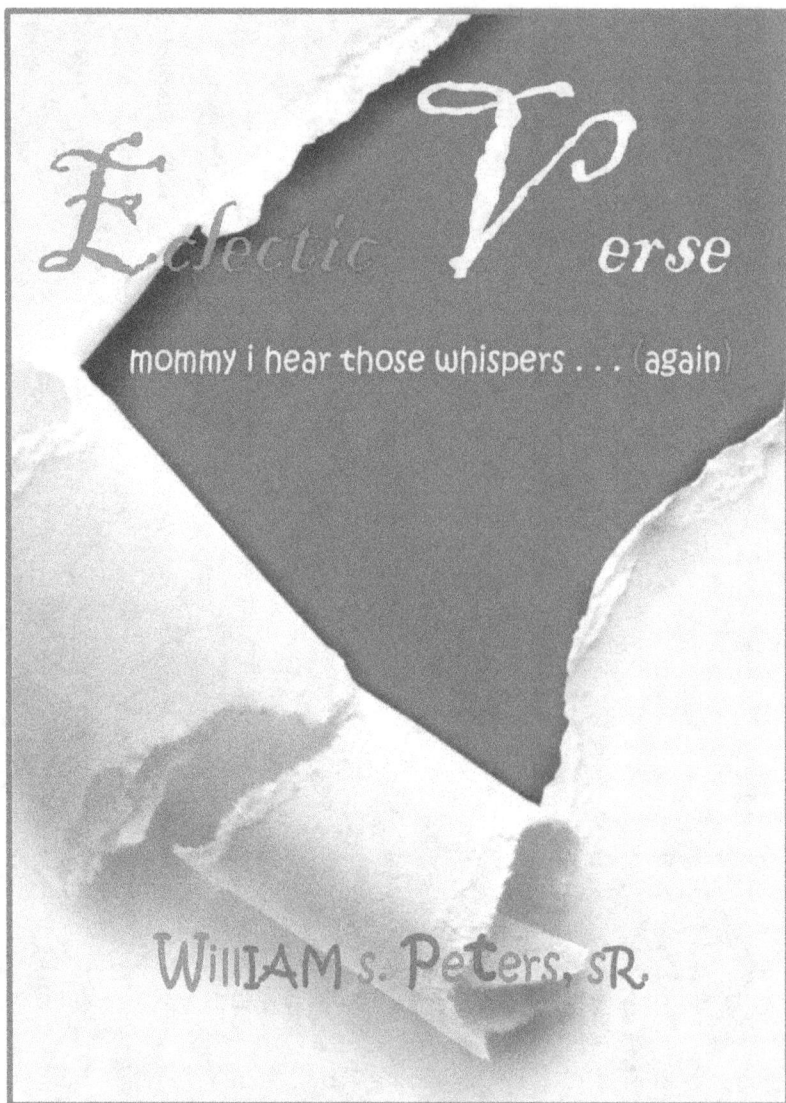

Eclectic Verse

mommy i hear those whispers . . . (again)

William S. Peters, Sr.

Now Available at
www.innerchildpress.com

HERENOW

FAHREDIN SHEHU

Now Available at
www.innerchildpress.com

Magnetic People

Eliza Segiet

Translated by Artur Komoter

Now Available at
www.innerchildpress.com

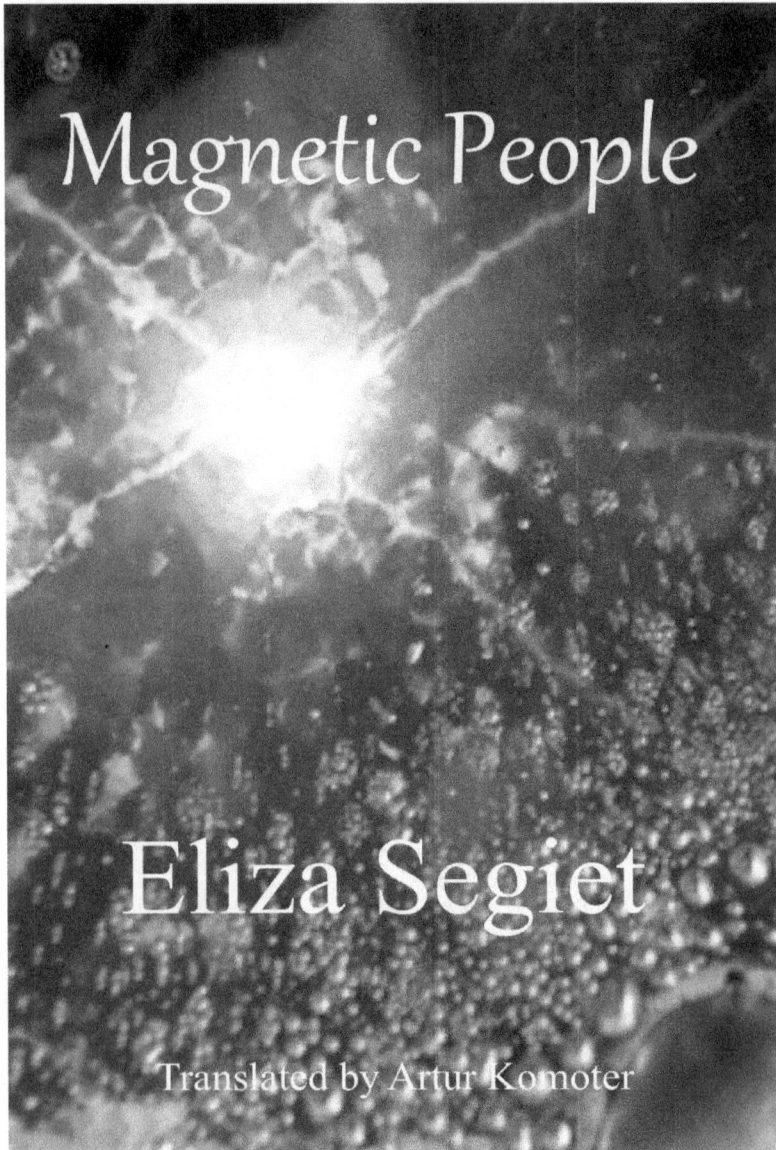

Dark Side

of the

Moon

Jackie Davis Allen

Now Available at
www.innerchildpress.com

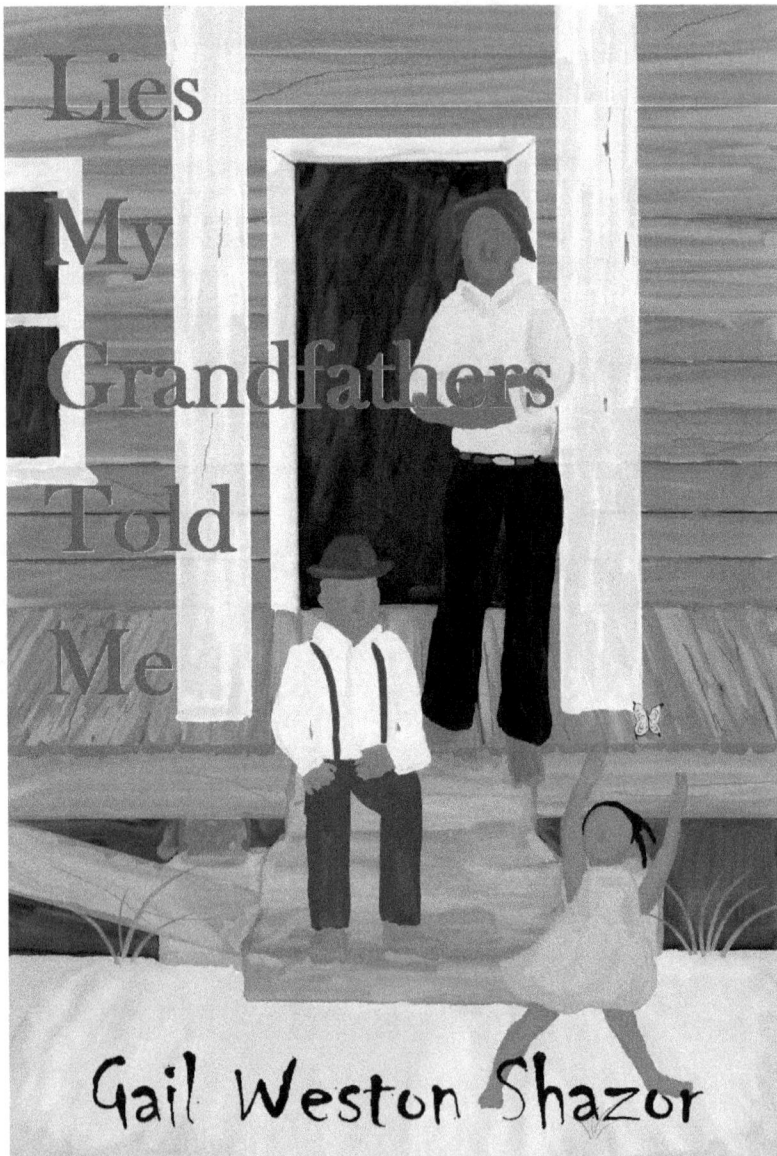

Lies My Grandfathers Told Me

Gail Weston Shazor

Now Available at
www.innerchildpress.com

Aflame

Memoirs in Verse

hülya n. yılmaz

Now Available at
www.innerchildpress.com

Now Available at

www.innerchildpress.com

Breakfast

for

Butterflies

Faleeha Hassan

Now Available at
www.innerchildpress.com

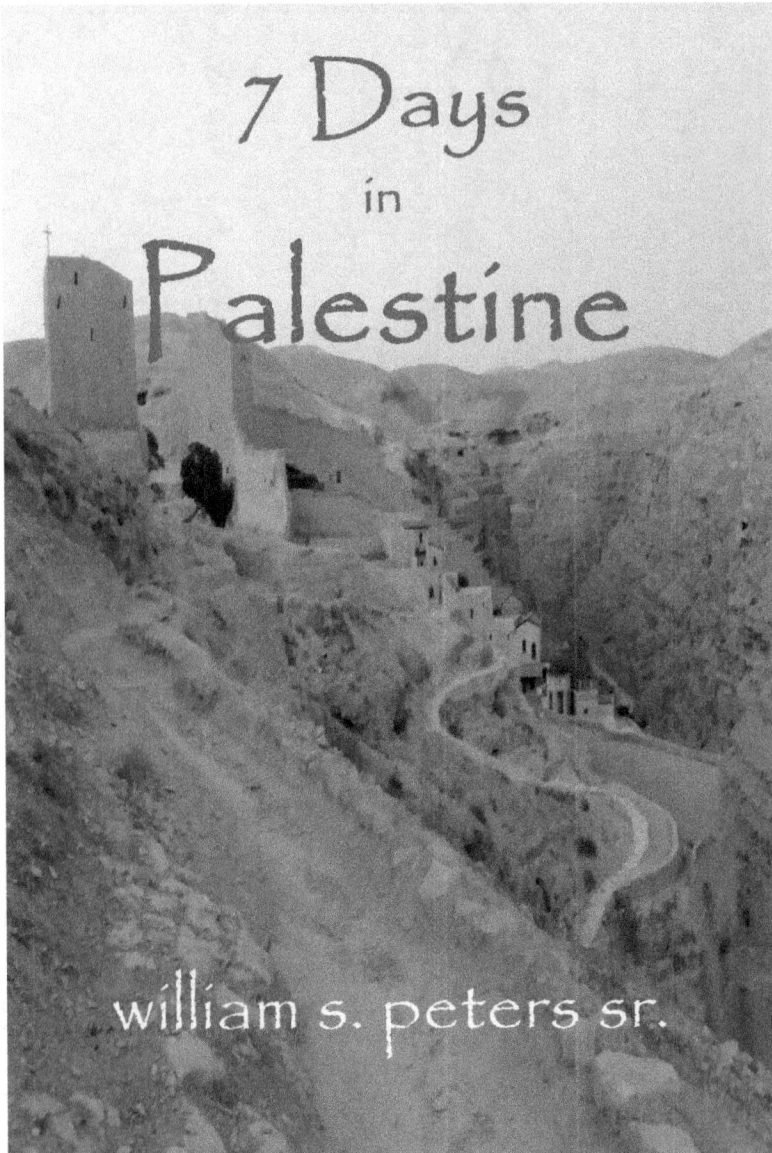

7 Days
in
Palestine

william s. peters sr.

Now Available at
www.innerchildpress.com

inner child press
presents

Tunisian Dreams

william s. peters, sr.

Now Available at
www.innerchildpress.com

INNER CHILD PRESS

THIS IS WHY I
SLEEP

william s. peters sr.

Now Available at
www.innerchildpress.com

Inward Reflections

Think on These Things
Book II

william s. peters, sr.

Now Available at
www.innerchildpress.com

my inner garden

~ expressions and discoveries ~

by

William S. Peters, Sr.

Now Available

www.innerchildpress.com

Other
Anthological
works from

Inner Child Press International

www.innerchildpress.com

Inner Child Press International

presents

W.A.R."

We Are Revolution

Too Much Blood

Poets for Humanity

Now Available

www.innerchildpress.com

I want my poetry to... *volume* 4

the conscious poets

inspired by . . . Monte Smith

Now Available

www.innerchildpress.com/anthologies

Now Available

www.innerchildpress.com/anthologies

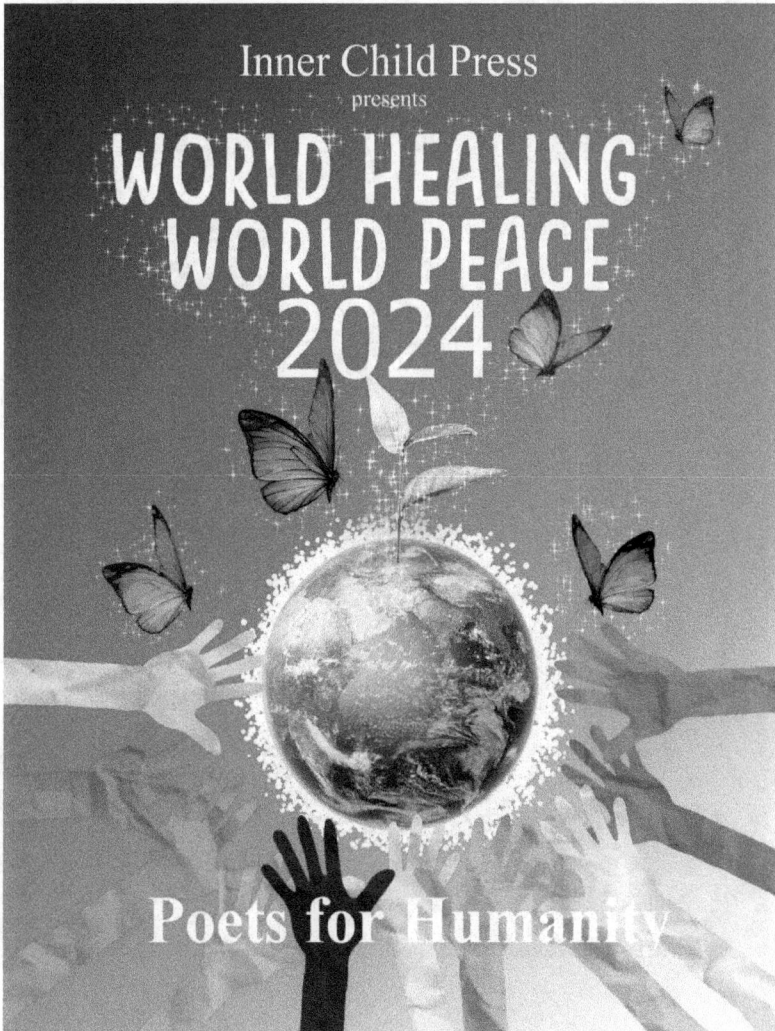

Inner Child Press
presents

**WORLD HEALING
WORLD PEACE
2024**

Poets for Humanity

Now Available

www.worldhealingworldpeacepoetry.com

World Healing World Peace 2022

Poets for Humanity

Now Available

www.innerchildpress.com/anthologies

World Healing World Peace
2020

Poets for Humanity

Now Available

www.worldhealingworldpeacepoetry.com

Now Available

www.innerchildpress.com/anthologies

Inner Child Press International
&
The Year of the Poet
present

Poetry

the best of 2020

Poets of the World

Now Available

www.innerchildpress.com/anthologies

Inner Child Press International

presents

W.A.R.

We Are Revolution

Poets for Humanity

Now Available

www.innerchildpress.com/anthologies

the Heart of a Poet

words for a better tomorrow

The Conscious Poets

Now Available

www.innerchildpress.com/anthologies

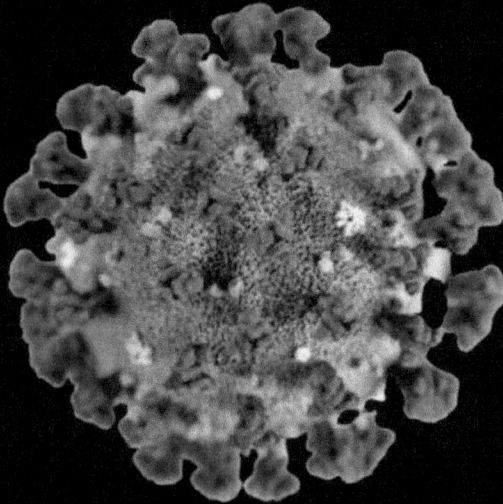

Corona

Social Distancing

Poets for Humanity

Now Available
www.innerchildpress.com/anthologies

Now Available

www.innerchildpress.com/anthologies

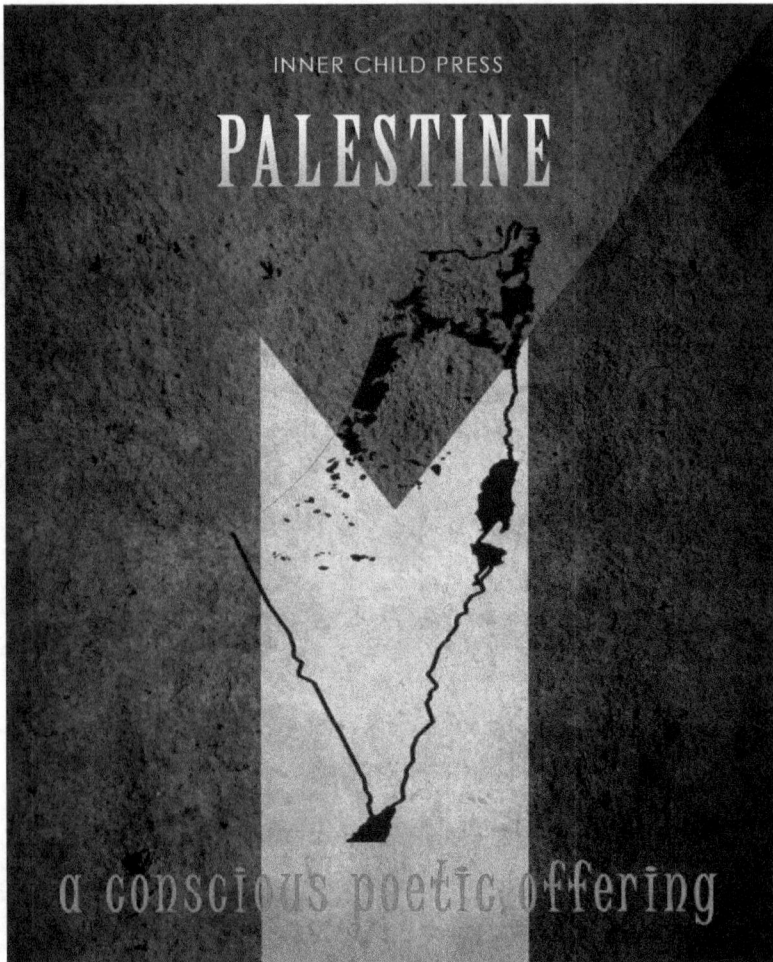

INNER CHILD PRESS

PALESTINE

a conscious poetic offering

Now Available
www.innerchildpress.com/anthologies

Now Available

www.innerchildpress.com/anthologies

Inner Child Press International
presents

A Love Anthology
2019

The Love Poets

Now Available
www.innerchildpress.com/anthologies

Now Available

www.worldhealingworldpeacepoetry.com

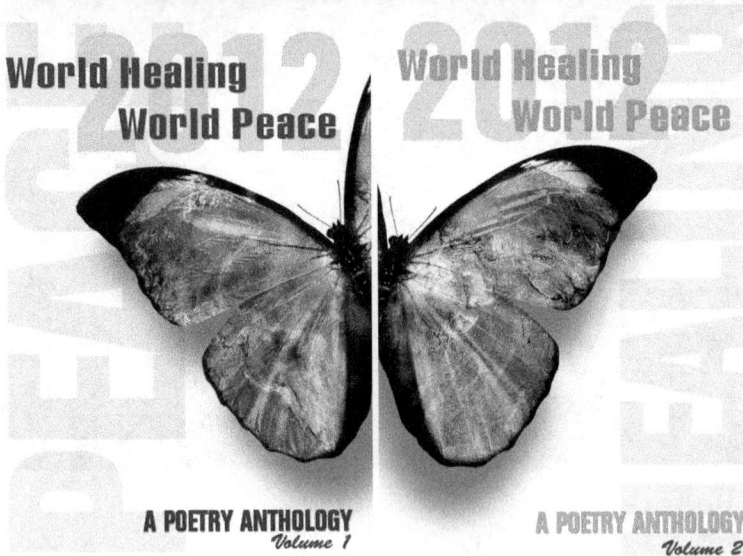

Now Available

www.worldhealingworldpeacepoetry.com

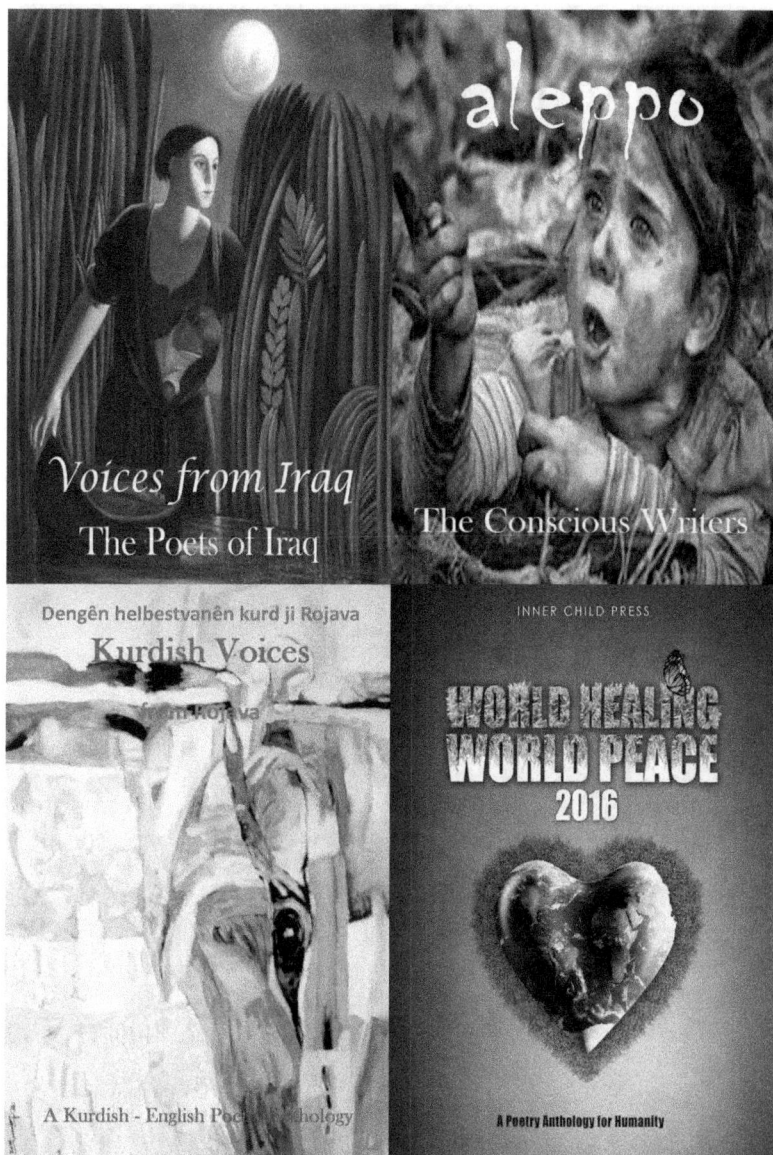

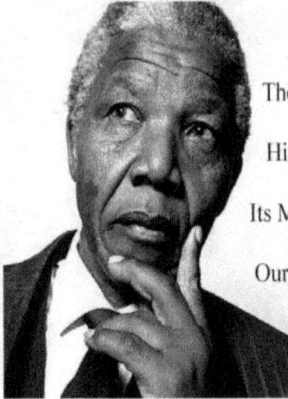

Mandela

The Man

His Life

Its Meaning

Our Words

Poetry . . . Commentary & Stories
The Anthological Writers

A GATHERING OF WORDS

POETRY & COMMENTARY
FOR
TRAYVON MARTIN

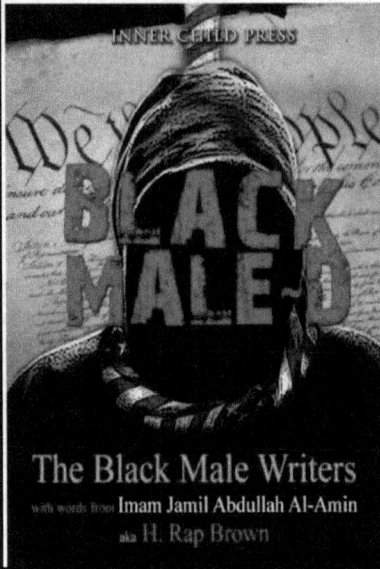

INNER CHILD PRESS

The Black Male Writers

with words from **Imam Jamil Abdullah Al-Amin**
aka H. Rap Brown

I want my poetry to... *volume* 4

the conscious poets

inspired by . . . Monte Smith

Now Available

www.innerchildpress.com/anthologies

a collection of the Voices of Many inspired by . . .

i ♥

want my

PoEtRy

to . . .

a collection of the Voices of Many inspired by . . .

Monte Smith

i ♥ Monte Smith

want my

PoEtRy

to . . .

volume II

i ♥

want my

PoEtRy

to . . . volume 3

a collection of the Voices of Many inspired by . . .

Monte Smith

11 Words

(9 lines . . .)

for those who are challenged

an anthology of Poetry inspired by . . .

Poetry Dancer

Now Available

www.innerchildpress.com/anthologies

The Year of the Poet
January 2014

The Poetry Posse

Jamie Bond
Gail Weston Shazor
Albert 'Infinite' Carrasco
Siddartha Beth Pierce
Janet P. Caldwell
June 'Bugg' Barefield
Debbie M. Allen
Tony Henninger
Joe DaVerbal Minddancer
Robert Gibbons
Neetu Wali
Shareef Abdur-Rasheed
William S. Peters, Sr.

Carnation

Our January Feature
Terri L. Johnson

the Year of the Poet
February 2014

violets

The Poetry Posse

Jamie Bond
Gail Weston Shazor
Albert 'Infinite' Carrasco
Siddartha Beth Pierce
Janet P. Caldwell
June 'Bugg' Barefield
Debbie M. Allen
Tony Henninger
Joe DaVerbal Minddancer
Robert Gibbons
Neetu Wali
Shareef Abdur-Rasheed
William S. Peters, Sr.

Our February Features
Teresa E. Gallion & Robert Gibson

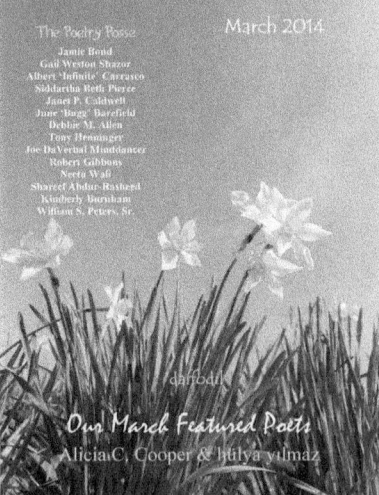

the Year of the Poet
March 2014

The Poetry Posse

Jamie Bond
Gail Weston Shazor
Albert 'Infinite' Carrasco
Siddartha Beth Pierce
Janet P. Caldwell
June 'Bugg' Barefield
Debbie M. Allen
Tony Henninger
Joe DaVerbal Minddancer
Robert Gibbons
Neetu Wali
Shareef Abdur-Rasheed
Kimberly Burnham
William S. Peters, Sr.

daffodil

Our March Featured Poets
Alicia C. Cooper & Hülya yılmaz

the Year of the Poet
April 2014

The Poetry Posse

Jamie Bond
Gail Weston Shazor
Albert 'Infinite' Carrasco
Siddartha Beth Pierce
Janet P. Caldwell
June 'Bugg' Barefield
Debbie M. Allen
Tony Henninger
Joe DaVerbal Minddancer
Robert Gibbons
Neetu Wali
Shareef Abdur-Rasheed
Kimberly Burnham
William S. Peters, Sr.

Our April Featured Poets
Fahredin Shehu
Martina Reisz Newberry
Justin Blackburn
Monte Smith

Sweet Pea

celebrating international poetry month

Now Available
www.innerchildpress.com/the-year-of-the-poet

the year of the poet

May 2014

May's Featured Poets

ReeCee
Joski the Poet
Shannon Stanton

Dedicated To our Children

The Poetry Posse

Jamie Bond
Gail Weston Shazor
Albert 'Infinite' Carrasco
Siddartha Beth Pierre
Janet P. Caldwell
June 'Bugg' Barefield
Debbie M. Allen
Fousy Hernandez
Joe DeVerbal 'Minddancer'
Robert Gibbons
Neetu Wali
Shareef Abdur-Rasheed
Kimberly Burnham
William S. Peters, Sr.

Lily of the Valley

the Year of the Poet

June 2014

Love & Relationship

Rose

June's Featured Poets

Shantelle McLin
Jacqueline D. E. Kennedy
Abraham N. Benjamin

The Poetry Posse

Jamie Bond
Gail Weston Shazor
Albert 'Infinite' Carrasco
Siddartha Beth Pierce
Janet P. Caldwell
June 'Bugg' Barefield
Debbie M. Allen
Tony Henninger
Joe DeVerbal Minddancer
Robert Gibbons
Neetu Wali
Shareef Abdur-Rasheed
Kimberly Burnham
William S. Peters, Sr.

The Year of the Poet

July 2014

July Feature Poets
Christena A. V. Williams
Dr. John R. Strum
Rolade Olanrewa5u Freedom

The Poetry Posse
Jamie Bond
Gail Weston Shazor

Siddartha Beth Pierce

June 'Bugg' Barefield
Debbie M. Allen
Tony Henninger
Joe DeVerbal Minddancer
Robert Gibbons
Neetu Wali
Shareef Abdur-Rasheed
Kimberly Burnham
William S. Peters, Sr.

Lotus
Asian Flower of the Month

The Year of the Poet

August 2014

Gladiolus

The Poetry Posse
Jamie Bond
Gail Weston Shazor
Albert 'Infinite' Carrasco
Siddartha Beth Pierce
Janet P. Caldwell
June 'Bugg' Barefield
Debbie M. Allen
Tony Henninger
Joe DeVerbal Minddancer
Robert Gibbons
Neetu Wali
Shareef Abdur-Rasheed
Kimberly Burnham
William S. Peters, Sr.

August Feature Poets

Ann White * Rosalind Cherry * Shelia Jenkins

Now Available

www.innerchildpress.com/the-year-of-the-poet

207

THE YEAR OF THE POET II
January 2015

Garnet

The Poetry Posse

Jamie Bond
Gail Weston Shazor
Albert 'Infinite' Carrasco
Siddartha Beth Pierce
Janet P. Caldwell
Tony Henninger
Joe DaVerbal Minddancer
Robert Gibbons
Neetu Wali
Shareef Abdur – Rasheed
Ann White
Keith Alan Hamilton
Katherine Wyatt
Fahredin Shehu
Hülya N. Yılmaz
Teresa E. Gallion
Jackie Allen
William S. Peters, Sr.

January Feature Poets
Bismay Mohanti * Jen Walls * Eric Judah

THE YEAR OF THE POET II
February 2015

Amethyst

THE POETRY POSSE

Jamie Bond
Gail Weston Shazor
Albert 'Infinite' Carrasco
Siddartha Beth Pierce
Janet P. Caldwell
Tony Henninger
Joe DaVerbal Minddancer
Robert Gibbons
Neetu Wali
Shareef Abdur – Rasheed
Kimberly Burnham
Ann White
Keith Alan Hamilton
Katherine Wyatt
Fahredin Shehu
Hülya N. Yılmaz
Teresa E. Gallion
Jackie Allen
William S. Peters, Sr.

FEBRUARY FEATURE POETS
Iram Fatima * Bob McNeil * Kerstin Centervall

The Year of the Poet II
March 2015

Our Featured Poets
Heung Sook * Anthony Arnold * Alicia Poland

Bloodstone

The Poetry Posse 2015
Jamie Bond * Gail Weston Shazor * Albert 'Infinite' Carrasco
Siddartha Beth Pierce * Janet P. Caldwell * Tony Henninger
Joe DaVerbal Minddancer * Neetu Wali * Shareef Abdur – Rasheed
Kimberly Burnham * Ann White * Keith Alan Hamilton
Katherine Wyatt * Fahredin Shehu * Hülya N. Yılmaz
Teresa E. Gallion * Jackie Allen * William S. Peters, Sr.

The Year of the Poet II
April 2015

Celebrating International Poetry Month

Our Featured Poets
Raja Williams * Dennis Ferado * Laure Charazac

Diamonds

The Poetry Posse 2015
Jamie Bond * Gail Weston Shazor * Albert 'Infinite' Carrasco
Siddartha Beth Pierce * Janet P. Caldwell * Tony Henninger
Joe DaVerbal Minddancer * Neetu Wali * Shareef Abdur – Rasheed
Kimberly Burnham * Ann White * Keith Alan Hamilton
Katherine Wyatt * Fahredin Shehu * Hülya N. Yılmaz
Teresa E. Gallion * Jackie Allen * William S. Peters, Sr.

Now Available

www.innerchildpress.com/the-year-of-the-poet

The Year of the Poet II
May 2015

May's Featured Poets

Geri Algeri
Akin Mosi Chinnery
Anna Jakubcza...

Emeralds

The Poetry Posse 2015
Jamie Bond * Gail Weston Shazor * Albert 'Infinite' Carrasco
Siddartha Beth Pierce * Janet P. Caldwell * Tony Henninger
Joe DaVerbal Minddancer * Neetu Wali * Shareef Abdur – Rasheed
Kimberly Burnham * Ann White * Keith Alan Hamilton
Katherine Wyatt * Fahredin Shehu * Hülya N. Yılmaz
Teresa E. Gallion * Jackie Allen * William S. Peters, Sr.

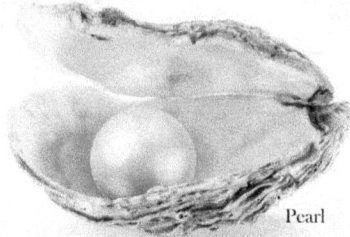

The Year of the Poet II
June 2015

June's Featured Poets

Anahit Arustamyan * Yvette D. Murrell * Regina A. Walker

Pearl

The Poetry Posse 2015
Jamie Bond * Gail Weston Shazor * Albert 'Infinite' Carrasco
Siddartha Beth Pierce * Janet P. Caldwell * Tony Henninger
Joe DaVerbal Minddancer * Neetu Wali * Shareef Abdur – Rasheed
Kimberly Burnham * Ann White * Keith Alan Hamilton
Katherine Wyatt * Fahredin Shehu * Hülya N. Yılmaz
Teresa E. Gallion * Jackie Allen * William S. Peters, Sr

The Year of the Poet II
July 2015

The Featured Poets for July 2015
Abhik Shome * Christina Neal * Robert Neal

Rubies

The Poetry Posse 2015
Jamie Bond * Gail Weston Shazor * Albert 'Infinite' Carrasco
Siddartha Beth Pierce * Janet P. Caldwell * Tony Henninger
Joe DaVerbal Minddancer * Neetu Wali * Shareef Abdur – Rasheed
Kimberly Burnham * Ann White * Keith Alan Hamilton
Katherine Wyatt * Fahredin Shehu * Hülya N. Yılmaz
Teresa E. Gallion * Jackie Allen * William S. Peters, Sr.

The Year of the Poet II
August 2015

Peridot

Featured Poets
Gayle Howell
Ann Chalasz
Christopher Schultz

The Poetry Posse 2015
Jamie Bond * Gail Weston Shazor * Albert 'Infinite' Carrasco
Siddartha Beth Pierce * Janet P. Caldwell * Tony Henninger
Joe DaVerbal Minddancer * Neetu Wali * Shareef Abdur – Rasheed
Kimberly Burnham * Ann White * Keith Alan Hamilton
Katherine Wyatt * Fahredin Shehu * Hülya N. Yılmaz
Teresa E. Gallion * Jackie Allen * William S. Peters, Sr

Now Available

www.innerchildpress.com/the-year-of-the-poet

The Year of the Poet II
Septiember 2015

Featured Poets
Alfreda Ghee * Lonneice Weeks Badley * Demetrios Trifiatis

Sapphires

The Poetry Posse 2015

Jamie Bond * Gail Weston Shazor * Albert 'Infinite' Carrasco
Siddartha Beth Pierce * Janet P. Caldwell * Tony Henninger
Joe DaVerbal Minddancer * Neetu Wali * Shareef Abdur – Rasheed
Kimberly Burnham * Ann White * Keith Alan Hamilton
Katherine Wyatt * Fahredin Shehu * Hülya N. Yılmaz
Teresa E. Gallion * Jackie Allen * William S. Peters. Sr.

The Year of the Poet II
October 2015

Featured Poets
Monte Smith * Laura J. Wolfe * William Washington

Opal

The Poetry Posse 2015

Jamie Bond * Gail Weston Shazor * Albert 'Infinite' Carrasco
Siddartha Beth Pierce * Janet P. Caldwell * Tony Henninger
Joe DaVerbal Minddancer * Neetu Wali * Shareef Abdur – Rasheed
Kimberly Burnham * Ann White * Keith Alan Hamilton
Katherine Wyatt * Fahredin Shehu * Hülya N. Yılmaz
Teresa E. Gallion * Jackie Allen * William S. Peters, Sr.

The Year of the Poet II
November 2015

Featured Poets
Alan W. Jankowski

Bismay Mohanty

James Moore

Topaz

The Poetry Posse 2015

Jamie Bond * Gail Weston Shazor * Albert 'Infinite' Carrasco
Siddartha Beth Pierce * Janet P. Caldwell * Tony Henninger
Joe DaVerbal Minddancer * Neetu Wali * Shareef Abdur – Rasheed
Kimberly Burnham * Ann White * Keith Alan Hamilton
Katherine Wyatt * Fahredin Shehu * Hülya N. Yılmaz
Teresa E. Gallion * Jackie Allen * William S. Peters, Sr.

The Year of the Poet II
December 2015

Featured Poets
Kerione Bryan * Michelle Joan Barulich * Neville Hiatt

Turquoise

The Poetry Posse 2015

Jamie Bond * Gail Weston Shazor * Albert 'Infinite' Carrasco
Siddartha Beth Pierce * Janet P. Caldwell * Tony Henninger
Joe DaVerbal Minddancer * Neetu Wali * Shareef Abdur – Rasheed
Kimberly Burnham * Ann White * Keith Alan Hamilton
Katherine Wyatt * Fahredin Shehu * Hülya N. Yılmaz
Teresa E. Gallion * Jackie Allen * William S. Peters, Sr.

Now Available
www.innerchildpress.com/the-year-of-the-poet

The Year of the Poet III
January 2016

Featured Poets
Lana Joseph * Atom Cyrus Rush * Christena Williams

Dark-eyed Junco

The Poetry Posse 2016
Gail Weston Shazor * Anna Jakubczak Vel Ratty Adalan * Ann J. White
Fahredin Shehu * Hrishikesh Padhye * Janet P. Caldwell
Joe DaVerbal Middleton * Shareef Abdur - Rasheed
Albert Carrasco * Kimberly Burnham * Keith Alan Hamilton
Hülya N. Yılmaz * Demetrios Trifiatis * Alan W. Jankowski
Teresa E. Gallion * Jackie Davis Allen * William S. Peters. Sr.

The Year of the Poet III
February 2016

Featured Poets
Anthony Arnold
Anna Chalasz
Alexandra Hawthorne

Puffin

The Poetry Posse 2016
Gail Weston Shazor * Joe DaVerbal Middleton * Alfredo Ghee
Fahredin Shehu * Hrishikesh Padhye * Janet P. Caldwell
Anna Jakubczak Vel Ratty Adalan * Shareef Abdur - Rasheed
Albert Carrasco * Kimberly Burnham * Ann J. White
Hülya N. Yılmaz * Demetrios Trifiatis * Alan W. Jankowski
Teresa E. Gallion * Jackie Davis Allen * William S. Peters. Sr.

The Year of the Poet III
March 2016

Featured Poets
Jeton Kelmendi   Nizar Sartawi   Sami Muhanna

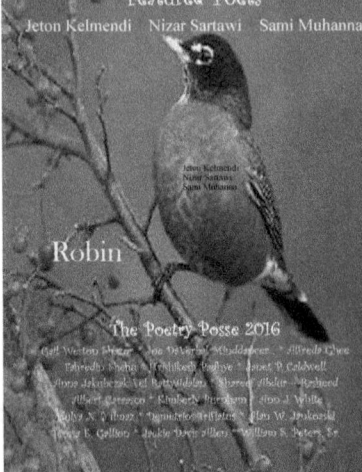

Robin

The Poetry Posse 2016
Gail Weston Shazor * Joe DaVerbal Middleton * Alfredo Ghee
Fahredin Shehu * Hrishikesh Padhye * Janet P. Caldwell
Anna Jakubczak Vel Ratty Adalan * Shareef Abdur - Rasheed
Albert Carrasco * Kimberly Burnham * Ann J. White
Hülya N. Yılmaz * Demetrios Trifiatis * Alan W. Jankowski
Teresa E. Gallion * Jackie Davis Allen * William S. Peters. Sr.

The Year of the Poet III

Featured Poets

Ali Abdolrezaei

Anna Chalasz

Agim Vinca

Ceri Naz

Black Capped Chickadee

The Poetry Posse 2016

Gail Weston Shazor * Joe DaVerbal Middleton * Alfredo Ghee
Fahredin Shehu * Hrishikesh Padhye * Janet P. Caldwell
Anna Jakubczak Vel Ratty Adalan * Shareef Abdur - Rasheed
Albert Carrasco * Kimberly Burnham * Ann J. White
Hülya N. Yılmaz * Demetrios Trifiatis * Alan W. Jankowski
Teresa E. Gallion * Jackie Davis Allen * William S. Peters. Sr.

celebrating international poetry month

Now Available

www.innerchildpress.com/the-year-of-the-poet

The Year of the Poet III — May 2016

Featured
Bob Strum
Barbara Allan
D.L. Davis

Oriole

The Poetry Posse 2016

The Year of the Poet III — June 2016

Featured Poets
Qibrije Demiri- Frangu
Naime Beqiraj
Faleeha Hassan
Bedri Zyberaj

Black Necked Stilt

The Poetry Posse 2016

The Year of the Poet III — July 2016

Featured Poets
Iram Fatima 'Ashi'
Langley Shazor
Jody Doty
Emilia T. Davis

Indigo Bunting

The Poetry Posse 2016

The Year of the Poet III — August 2016

Featured Poets
Anita Dash
Irena Jovanovic
Malgorzata Gouluda

Painted Bunting

The Poetry Posse 2016

Now Available

www.innerchildpress.com/the-year-of-the-poet

213

The Year of the Poet III — September 2016
Featured Poets: Simone Weber, Abhijit Sen, Eunice Barbara C. Novio
Long Billed Curle
The Poetry Posse 2016

The Year of the Poet III — October 2016
Featured Poets: Lana Joseph, a Krishnamurthy, James Moore
Barn Owl
The Poetry Posse 2016

The Year of the Poet III — November 2016
Featured Poets: Rosemary Burns, Robin Ouzman Hislop, Lonneice Weeks-Badley
Northern Cardinal
The Poetry Posse 2016

The Year of the Poet III — December 2016
Featured Poets: Samih Masoud, Mountassir Aziz Bien, Abdulkadir Musa
Rough Legged Hawk
The Poetry Posse 2016

Now Available

www.innerchildpress.com/the-year-of-the-poet

The Year of the Poet IV
January 2017

Featured Poets

Jon Winell
Natalie Shields
Iftani Fatima "Ashi

Quaking Aspen

The Poetry Posse 2017

Gail Weston Shazor * Caroline Nazareno * Blamey Mohanty
Nizar Sartawi * Anna Jakubczak Vel Ratty Adalan * Jen Walls
Joe DaVerbal Minddancer * Shareef Abdur - Rasheed
Albert Carrasco * Kimberly Burnham * Elizabeth Castillo
Hülya N. Yılmaz * Faleeha Hassan * Alan W. Jankowski
Teresa E. Gallion * Jackie Davis Allen * William S. Peters, Sr.

The Year of the Poet IV
February 2017

Featured Poets

Lin Ross
Soukaina Fathi
Anwer Ghani

Witch Hazel

The Poetry Posse 2017

Gail Weston Shazor * Caroline Nazareno * Blamey Mohanty
Nizar Sartawi * Anna Jakubczak Vel Ratty Adalan * Jen Walls
Joe DaVerbal Minddancer * Shareef Abdur - Rasheed
Albert Carrasco * Kimberly Burnham * Elizabeth Castillo
Hülya N. Yılmaz * Faleeha Hassan * Alan W. Jankowski
Teresa E. Gallion * Jackie Davis Allen * William S. Peters, Sr.

The Year of the Poet IV
March 2017

Featured Poets

Tremell Stevens
Francisca Ricinski
Jamil Abu Shaih

The Eastern Redbud

The Poetry Posse 2017

Gail Weston Shazor * Caroline Nazareno * Blamey Mohanty
Teresa E. Gallion * Anna Jakubczak Vel Ratty Adalan
Joe DaVerbal Minddancer * Shareef Abdur - Rasheed
Albert Carrasco * Kimberly Burnham * Elizabeth Castillo
Hülya N. Yılmaz * Faleeha Hassan * Jackie Davis Allen
Jen Walls * Nizar Sartawi * * William S. Peters, Sr.

The Year of the Poet IV
April 2017

Featured Poets

Dr. Rachida Barman
Neptune Barman
Masoud Khalaf

The Blossoming Cherry

The Poetry Posse 2017

Gail Weston Shazor * Caroline Nazareno * Blamey Mohanty
Teresa E. Gallion * Anna Jakubczak Vel Ratty Adalan
Joe DaVerbal Minddancer * Shareef Abdur - Rasheed
Albert Carrasco * Kimberly Burnham * Elizabeth Castillo
Hülya N. Yılmaz * Faleeha Hassan * Jackie Davis Allen
Jen Walls * Nizar Sartawi * * William S. Peters, Sr.

Now Available

www.innerchildpress.com/the-year-of-the-poet

The Year of the Poet IV
May 2017

The Flowering Dogwood Tree

Featured Poets
Kallisa Powell
Alicja Maria Kuberska
Fethi Sassi

The Poetry Posse 2017

Gail Weston Shazor * Caroline Nazareno * Jhimmy Mohanty
Teresa E. Gallion * Anna Jakubczak Vel Ratty Adalan
Joe DaVerbal Minddancer * Shareef Abdur - Rasheed
Albert Carrasco * Kimberly Burnham * Elizabeth Castillo
Hülya N. Yılmaz * Faleeha Hassan * Jackie Davis Allen
Jen Walls * Nizar Sartawi * * William S. Peters, Sr.

The Year of the Poet IV
June 2017

Featured Poets
Eliza Segiet
Tze-Min Tsai
Abdulla Issa

The Linden Tree

The Poetry Posse 2017

Gail Weston Shazor... Jhimmy Mohanty
...
Hülya N. Yılmaz * ... * Jackie Davis Allen
Jen Walls * Nizar Sartawi * William S. Peters, Sr.

The Year of the Poet IV
July 2017

Featured Poets
Anca Mihaela Bruma
Ibaa Ismail
Zvonko Taneski

The Oak Moon

The Poetry Posse 2017

Gail Weston Shazor * Caroline Nazareno * Jhimmy Mohanty
Teresa E. Gallion * Anna Jakubczak Vel Ratty Adalan
Joe DaVerbal Minddancer * Shareef Abdur - Rasheed
Albert Carrasco * Kimberly Burnham * Elizabeth Castillo
Hülya N. Yılmaz * Faleeha Hassan * Jackie Davis Allen
Jen Walls * Nizar Sartawi * * William S. Peters, Sr.

The Year of the Poet IV
August 2017

Featured Poets
Jonathan Aquino
Kitty Hsu
Langley Shazor

The Hazelnut Tree

The Poetry Posse 2017

Gail Weston Shazor * Caroline Nazareno *
Teresa E. Gallion * Anna Jakubczak Vel Ratty Adalan
Joe DaVerbal Minddancer * Shareef Abdur - Rasheed
Albert Carrasco * Kimberly Burnham * Elizabeth Castillo
Hülya N. Yılmaz * Faleeha Hassan * Jackie Davis Allen
Jen Walls * Nizar Sartawi * * William S. Peters, Sr.

Now Available

www.innerchildpress.com/the-year-of-the-poet

The Year of the Poet IV
September 2017

Featured Poets

Martina Reisz Newberry
Ameer Nassir
Christine Fulco Neal
Robert Neal

The Elm Tree

The Poetry Posse 2017

Gail Weston Shazor * Caroline Nazareno * Bismay Mohanty
Teresa E. Gallion * Anna Jakubczak Vel Ratty Adalan
Joe DaVerbal Minddancer * Shareef Abdur – Rasheed
Albert Carrasco * Kimberly Burnham * Elizabeth Castillo
Hülya N. Yılmaz * Faleeha Hassan * Jackie Davis Allen
Jen Walls * Nizar Sartawi * * William S. Peters, Sr.

The Year of the Poet IV
October 2017

Featured Poets

Ahmed Abu Saleem
Nedal Al-Qaeim
Sadeddin Shahin

The Black Walnut Tree

The Poetry Posse 2017

Gail Weston Shazor * Caroline Nazareno * Bismay Mohanty
Teresa E. Gallion * Anna Jakubczak Vel Ratty Adalan
Joe DaVerbal Minddancer * Shareef Abdur – Rasheed
Albert Carrasco * Kimberly Burnham * Elizabeth Castillo
Hülya N. Yılmaz * Faleeha Hassan * Jackie Davis Allen
Jen Walls * Nizar Sartawi * * William S. Peters, Sr.

The Year of the Poet IV
November 2017

Featured Poets

Kay Peters
Alfreda D. Ghee
Gabriella Garofalo
Rosemary Cappello

The Tree of Life

The Poetry Posse 2017

Gail Weston Shazor * Caroline Nazareno * Bismay Mohanty
Teresa E. Gallion * Anna Jakubczak Vel Ratty Adalan
Joe DaVerbal Minddancer * Shareef Abdur – Rasheed
Albert Carrasco * Kimberly Burnham * Elizabeth Castillo
Hülya N. Yılmaz * Faleeha Hassan * Jackie Davis Allen
Jen Walls * Nizar Sartawi * William S. Peters, Sr.

The Year of the Poet IV
December 2017

Featured Poets

Justice Clarke
Mariel M. Pabroa
Kiley Brown

The Fig Tree

The Poetry Posse 2017

Gail Weston Shazor * Caroline Nazareno * Bismay Mohanty
Teresa E. Gallion * Anna Jakubczak Vel Ratty Adalan
Joe DaVerbal Minddancer * Shareef Abdur – Rasheed
Albert Carrasco * Kimberly Burnham * Elizabeth Castillo
Hülya N. Yılmaz * Faleeha Hassan * Jackie Davis Allen
Jen Walls * Nizar Sartawi * William S. Peters, Sr.

Now Available
www.innerchildpress.com/the-year-of-the-poet

217

The Year of the Poet V
January 2018
Featured Poets

Iyad Shamasnah
Yasmeen Hamzeh
Ali Abdolrezaei

Aksum

The Poetry Posse 2018
Gail Weston Shazor * Caroline Nazareno * Tezmin Ition Tsai
Hülya N. Yılmaz * Faleeha Hassan * Jackie Davis Allen
Teresa E. Gallion * Anna Jakubczak Vel Ratty Adalan
Alicja Maria Kuberska * Shareef Abdur – Rasheed
Kimberly Burnham * Elizabeth Castillo
Nizar Sartawi * William S. Peters, Sr.

The Year of the Poet V
February 2018

Sabean

Featured Poets
Muhammad Azram
Anna Szawracka
Abhilipsa Kuanar
Aanika Aery

The Poetry Posse 2018
Gail Weston Shazor * Caroline Nazareno * Tezmin Ition Tsai
Hülya N. Yılmaz * Faleeha Hassan * Jackie Davis Allen
Teresa E. Gallion * Anna Jakubczak Vel Ratty Adalan
Alicja Maria Kuberska * Shareef Abdur – Rasheed
Kimberly Burnham * Elizabeth Castillo
Nizar Sartawi * William S. Peters, Sr.

The Year of the Poet V
March 2018

Featured Poets
Irasn Fatima 'Ashi'
Cassandra Swan
Jaleel Khazaal
Shazia Zaman

Caribbean
&
Middle America

The Poetry Posse 2018
Gail Weston Shazor * Nizar Sartawi * Hülya N. Yılmaz
Jackie Davis Allen * Caroline 'Ceri' Nazareno
Alicja Maria Kuberska * Teresa E. Gallion
Faleeha Hassan * Shareef Abdur – Rasheed
Kimberly Burnham * Elizabeth Castillo
Tezmin Ition Tsai * William S. Peters, Sr.

The Year of the Poet V
April 2018

Featured Poets

The Nez Perce

The Poetry Posse 2018

Now Available
www.innerchildpress.com/the-year-of-the-poet

The Year of the Poet V
May 2018

Featured Poets

Zakly Carreón de León Jr.
Sylwia K. Malinowska
Lindita Ahmeti
Ofelia Prodan

The Sumerians

The Poetry Posse 2018

Gail Weston Shazor * Nizar Sartawi * Hülya N. Yılmaz
Jackie Davis Allen * Caroline 'Ceri' Nazareno
Alicja Maria Kubenska * Teresa E. Gallion
Kimberly Burnham * Shareef Abdur – Rasheed
Faleeha Hassan * Elizabeth Castillo * Swapna Behera
Tezmin Ition Tsai * William S. Peters, Sr.

The Year of the Poet V
June 2018

Featured Poets

Bilall Maliqi * Daim Miftari * Gojko Božović * Sofija Živković

The Paleo Indians

The Poetry Posse 2018

Gail Weston Shazor * Nizar Sartawi * Hülya N. Yılmaz
Jackie Davis Allen * Caroline 'Ceri' Nazareno
Alicja Maria Kubenska * Teresa E. Gallion
Kimberly Burnham * Shareef Abdur – Rasheed
Faleeha Hassan * Elizabeth Castillo * Swapna Behera
Tezmin Ition Tsai * William S. Peters, Sr.

The Year of the Poet V
July 2018

Featured Poets

Fatimah Irengar-Padde
Mohammad Bilal Hamid
Eliza Segiet
Tom Higgins

Oceania

The Poetry Posse 2018

Gail Weston Shazor * Nizar Sartawi * Hülya N. Yılmaz
Jackie Davis Allen * Caroline 'Ceri' Nazareno
Alicja Maria Kubenska * Teresa E. Gallion
Kimberly Burnham * Shareef Abdur – Rasheed
Faleeha Hassan * Elizabeth Castillo * Swapna Behera
Tezmin Ition Tsai * William S. Peters, Sr.

The Year of the Poet V
August 2018

Featured Poets

Hussein Habasch * Mircea Dan Duta * Naida Mujkić * Swagat Das

The Lapita

The Poetry Posse 2018

Gail Weston Shazor * Nizar Sartawi * Hülya N. Yılmaz
Jackie Davis Allen * Caroline 'Ceri' Nazareno
Alicja Maria Kubenska * Teresa E. Gallion
Kimberly Burnham * Shareef Abdur – Rasheed
Ashok K. Bhargava * Elizabeth Castillo * Swapna Behaera
Tezmin Ition Tsai * William S. Peters, Sr.

Now Available

www.innerchildpress.com/the-year-of-the-poet

The Year of the Poet V
September 2018

The Aztecs & Incas

Featured Poets
Kolade Olanrewaju Freedom
Eliza Segiet
Mazhar Hussain Abdul Ghori
Lily Swarn

The Poetry Posse 2018
Gail Weston Shazor * Nizar Sartawi * Hülya N. Yılmaz
Jackie Davis Allen * Caroline 'Ceri' Nazareno
Alicia Maria Kubersla * Teresa E. Gallion
Kimberly Burnham * Shareef Abdur – Rasheed
Ashok K. Bhargava * Elizabeth Castillo * Swapna Behera
Tezmin Ition Tsai * William S. Peters, Sr.

The Year of the Poet V
October 2018

Featured Poets
Alicia Minjarez * Lonneice Weeks-Badley
Lopamudra Mishra * Abdelwahed Souayah

Bengali

The Poetry Posse 2018
Gail Weston Shazor * Nizar Sartawi * Hülya N. Yılmaz
Jackie Davis Allen * Caroline 'Ceri' Nazareno
Alicia Maria Kubersla * Teresa E. Gallion
Kimberly Burnham * Shareef Abdur – Rasheed
Ashok K. Bhargava * Elizabeth Castillo * Swapna Behera
Tezmin Ition Tsai * William S. Peters, Sr.

The Year of the Poet V
November 2018

Featured Poets
Michelle Joan Barulich * Monsif Beroual
Krystyna Konecka * Nassira Nezzar

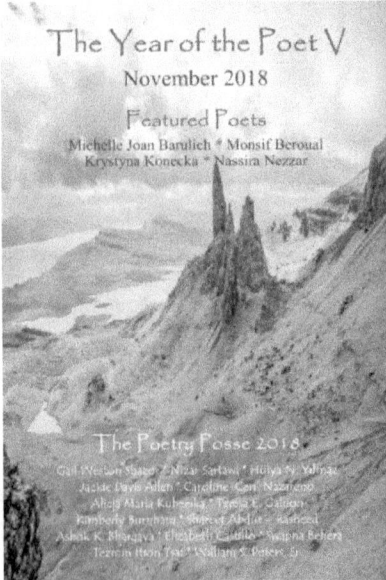

The Poetry Posse 2018
Gail Weston Shazor * Nizar Sartawi * Hülya N. Yılmaz
Jackie Davis Allen * Caroline 'Ceri' Nazareno
Alicia Maria Kubersla * Teresa E. Gallion
Kimberly Burnham * Shareef Abdur – Rasheed
Ashok K. Bhargava * Elizabeth Castillo * Swapna Behera
Tezmin Ition Tsai * William S. Peters, Sr.

The Year of the Poet V
December 2018

Featured Poets
Rose Terranova Cirigliano
Joanna Kalinowska
Sokolović Emin
Dr. T. Ashok Chakravarthy

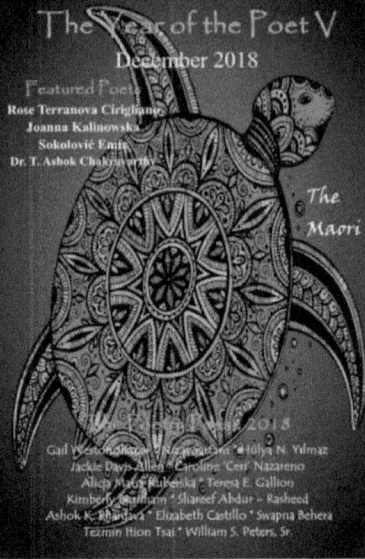

The Maori

The Poetry Posse 2018
Gail Weston Shazor * Nizar Sartawi * Hülya N. Yılmaz
Jackie Davis Allen * Caroline 'Ceri' Nazareno
Alicia Maria Kubersla * Teresa E. Gallion
Kimberly Burnham * Shareef Abdur – Rasheed
Ashok K. Bhargava * Elizabeth Castillo * Swapna Behera
Tezmin Ition Tsai * William S. Peters, Sr.

Now Available

www.innerchildpress.com/the-year-of-the-poet

The Year of the Poet VI

January 2019

Indigenous North Americans

Featured Poets

Houda Elfchtall
Anthony Briscoe
Iram Fatima 'Ashi'
Dr. K. K. Mathew

Dream Catcher

The Poetry Posse 2019

Gail Weston Shazor * Joe Paire * Hülya N. Yılmaz
Jackie Davis Allim * Caroline 'Ceri' Nazareno
Alicja Maria Kubeńska * Teresa E. Gallion
Kimberly Burnham * Shareef Abdur – Rasheed
Ashok K. Bhargava * Elizabeth Castillo * Swapna Behera
Tezmin Ition Tsai * William S. Peters, Sr.

The Year of the Poet VI

February 2019

Featured Poets

Marek Lukaszewicz * Bharati Nayak
Aida G. Roque * Jean-Jacques Fournier

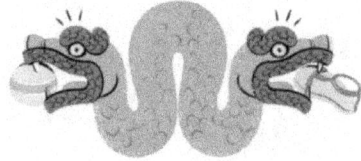

Meso-America

The Poetry Posse 2019

Gail Weston Shazor * Albert Carrasco * Hülya N. Yılmaz
Jackie Davis Allen * Caroline Nazareno * Eliza Segiet
Alicja Maria Kubeńska * Teresa E. Gallion * Joe Paire
Kimberly Burnham * Shareef Abdur – Rasheed
Ashok K. Bhargava * Elizabeth Castillo * Swapna Behera
Tezmin Ition Tsai * William S. Peters, Sr.

The Year of the Poet VI

March 2019

Featured Poets

Enesa Mahmić * Sylwia K. Malinowska
Shurouk Hammoud * Anwer Ghani

The Caribbean

The Poetry Posse 2019

Gail Weston Shazor * Albert Carrasco * Hülya N. Yılmaz
Jackie Davis Allen * Caroline Nazareno * Eliza Segiet
Alicja Maria Kubeńska * Teresa E. Gallion * Joe Paire
Kimberly Burnham * Shareef Abdur – Rasheed
Ashok K. Bhargava * Elizabeth Castillo * Swapna Behera
Tezmin Ition Tsai * William S. Peters, Sr.

The Year of the Poet VI

April 2019

Featured Poets

Dt. Davis * Michelle Joan Barulich
Lulëzim Haziri * Faleeha Hassan

Central & West Africa

The Poetry Posse 2019

Gail Weston Shazor * Albert Carrasco * Hülya N. Yılmaz
Jackie Davis Allen * Caroline Nazareno * Eliza Segiet
Alicja Maria Kubeńska * Teresa E. Gallion * Joe Paire
Kimberly Burnham * Shareef Abdur – Rasheed
Ashok K. Bhargava * Elizabeth Castillo * Swapna Behera
Tezmin Ition Tsai * William S. Peters, Sr.

Now Available

www.innerchildpress.com/the-year-of-the-poet

The Year of the Poet VI
May 2019

Featured Poets
Emad Al-Haydary * Hussein Nasser Jabr
Wahab Sheriff * Abdul Razzaq Al-Ameeri

Asia Southeast Asia and Maritime Asia

The Poetry Posse 2019

Gail Weston Shazor * Albert Carrasco * Hülya N. Yılmaz
Jackie Davis Allen * Caroline Nazareno * Eliza Segiet
Alicja Maria Kuberska * Teresa E. Gallion * Joe Paire
Kimberly Burnham * Shareef Abdur – Rasheed
Ashok K. Bhargava * Elizabeth Castillo * Swapna Behera
Tezmin Ition Tsai * William S. Peters, Sr.

The Year of the Poet VI
June 2019

Featured Poets
Kate Gaudi Powiekszone * Sahaj Sabharwal
Iwu Jeff * Mohamed Abdel Aziz Shmeis

Arctic
Circumpolar

The Poetry Posse 2019

Gail Weston Shazor * Albert Carrasco * Hülya N. Yılmaz
Jackie Davis Allen * Caroline Nazareno * Eliza Segiet
Alicja Maria Kuberska * Teresa E. Gallion * Joe Paire
Kimberly Burnham * Shareef Abdur – Rasheed
Ashok K. Bhargava * Elizabeth Castillo * Swapna Behera
Tezmin Ition Tsai * William S. Peters, Sr.

The Year of the Poet VI
July 2019

Featured Poets
Saadeddin Shahin   Andy Scott
Esheredin Shehu   Alok Kumar Ray

The Horn of Africa

Ethiopia   Djibouti

Somalia   Eritrea

The Poetry Posse 2019

Gail Weston Shazor * Albert Carrasco * Hülya N. Yılmaz
Jackie Davis Allen * Caroline Nazareno * Eliza Segiet
Alicja Maria Kuberska * Teresa E. Gallion * Joe Paire
Kimberly Burnham * Shareef Abdur – Rasheed
Ashok K. Bhargava * Elizabeth Castillo * Swapna Behera
Tezmin Ition Tsai * William S. Peters, Sr.

The Year of the Poet VI
August 2019

Featured Poets
Shola Balogun * Bharati Nayak
Monalisa Dash Dwibedy * Mbizo Chirasha

Coexist

Southwest Asia

The Poetry Posse 2019

Gail Weston Shazor * Albert Carrasco * Hülya N. Yılmaz
Jackie Davis Allen * Caroline Nazareno * Eliza Segiet
Alicja Maria Kuberska * Teresa E. Gallion * Joe Paire
Kimberly Burnham * Shareef Abdur – Rasheed
Ashok K. Bhargava * Elizabeth Castillo * Swapna Behera
Tezmin Ition Tsai * William S. Peters, Sr.

Now Available
www.innerchildpress.com/the-year-of-the-poet

The Year of the Poet VI

September 2019

Featured Poets

Elena Liliana Popescu * Gobinda Biswas
Iram Fatima 'Ashi' * Joseph S. Spence, Sr.

The Caucasus

The Poetry Posse 2019

Carl Weston Shazor * Albert Carrasco * Hülya N. Yılmaz
Jackie Davis Allen * Caroline Nazareno * Eliza Segiet
Alicja Maria Kuberska * Teresa E. Gallion * Joe Paire
Kimberly Burnham * Shareef Abdur – Rasheed
Ashok K. Bhargava * Elizabeth Castillo * Swapna Behera
Tezmin Ition Tsai * William S. Peters, Sr.

The Year of the Poet VI

October 2019

Featured Poets

Ngozi Olivia Osuoha * Denisa Kondic
Pankhuri Sinha * Christena AV Williams

The Nile Valley

The Poetry Posse 2019

Carl Weston Shazor * Albert Carrasco * Hülya N. Yılmaz
Jackie Davis Allen * Caroline Nazareno * Eliza Segiet
Alicja Maria Kuberska * Teresa E. Gallion * Joe Paire
Kimberly Burnham * Shareef Abdur – Rasheed
Ashok K. Bhargava * Elizabeth Castillo * Swapna Behera
Tezmin Ition Tsai * William S. Peters, Sr.

The Year of the Poet VI

November 2019

Featured Poets

Rozalia Aleksandrova * Gobindo Ganga
Smruti Ranjan Mohanty * Sofia Skleida

Northern Asia

The Poetry Posse 2019

Carl Weston Shazor * Albert Carrasco * Hülya N. Yılmaz
Jackie Davis Allen * Caroline Nazareno * Eliza Segiet
Alicja Maria Kuberska * Teresa E. Gallion * Joe Paire
Kimberly Burnham * Shareef Abdur – Rasheed
Ashok K. Bhargava * Elizabeth Castillo * Swapna Behera
Tezmin Ition Tsai * William S. Peters, Sr.

The Year of the Poet VI

December 2019

Featured Poets

Ramón Kirties (Kordován) * Sunny Paul
Bharat Nayak * Kapardeli Eftichia

Oceania

The Poetry Posse 2019

Carl Weston Shazor * Albert Carrasco * Hülya N. Yılmaz
Jackie Davis Allen * Caroline Nazareno * Eliza Segiet
Alicja Maria Kuberska * Teresa E. Gallion * Joe Paire
Kimberly Burnham * Shareef Abdur – Rasheed
Ashok K. Bhargava * Elizabeth Castillo * Swapna Behera
Tezmin Ition Tsai * William S. Peters, Sr.

Now Available

www.innerchildpress.com/the-year-of-the-poet

The Year of the Poet VII

January 2020

Featured Poets

B S Tyagi * Ashok Chakravarthy Tholana
Andy Scott * Anwer Ghani

1901 Jean Henry Dunant and Frédéric Passy

The Year of Peace
Celebrating past Nobel Peace Prize Recipients

The Poetry Posse 2020

Gail Weston Shazor * Albert Carasco * Hülya N. Yılmaz
Jackie Davis Allen * Caroline Nazareno * Eliza Segiet
Alicja Maria Kuberska * Teresa E. Gallion * Joe Paire
Kimberly Burnham * Shareef Abdur – Rasheed
Ashok K. Bhargava * Elizabeth Castillo * Swapna Behera
Tezmin Ition Tsai * William S. Peters, Sr.

The Year of the Poet VII

February 2020

Featured Poets

Jennifer Ades * Martina Reisz Newberry
Ibrahim Honjo * Claudia Piccinno

Henri La Fontaine ~ 1913

The Year of Peace
Celebrating past Nobel Peace Prize Recipients

The Poetry Posse 2020

Gail Weston Shazor * Albert Carasco * Hülya N. Yılmaz
Jackie Davis Allen * Caroline Nazareno * Eliza Segiet
Alicja Maria Kuberska * Teresa E. Gallion * Joe Paire
Kimberly Burnham * Shareef Abdur – Rasheed
Ashok K. Bhargava * Elizabeth Castillo * Swapna Behera
Tezmin Ition Tsai * William S. Peters, Sr.

The Year of the Poet VII

March 2020

Featured Poets

Aziz Mountassir * Krishna Paraisa
Hannie Rouweler * Rozalia Aleksandrova

Aristide Briand ~ 1926 ~ Gustav Stresemann

The Year of Peace
Celebrating past Nobel Peace Prize Recipients

The Poetry Posse 2020

Gail Weston Shazor * Albert Carasco * Hülya N. Yılmaz
Jackie Davis Allen * Caroline Nazareno * Eliza Segiet
Alicja Maria Kuberska * Teresa E. Gallion * Joe Paire
Kimberly Burnham * Shareef Abdur – Rasheed
Ashok K. Bhargava * Elizabeth Castillo * Swapna Behera
Tezmin Ition Tsai * William S. Peters, Sr.

The Year of the Poet VII

April 2020

Featured Poets

Rohini Behera * Mircea Dan Duta
Monalisa Dash Dwibedy * NilavroNill Shoovro

Carlos Saavedra Lamas ~ 1936

The Year of Peace
Celebrating past Nobel Peace Prize Recipients

The Poetry Posse 2020

Gail Weston Shazor * Albert Carasco * Hülya N. Yılmaz
Jackie Davis Allen * Caroline Nazareno * Eliza Segiet
Alicja Maria Kuberska * Teresa E. Gallion * Joe Paire
Kimberly Burnham * Shareef Abdur – Rasheed
Ashok K. Bhargava * Elizabeth Castillo * Swapna Behera
Tezmin Ition Tsai * William S. Peters, Sr.

Now Available

www.innerchildpress.com/the-year-of-the-poet

The Year of the Poet VII
May 2020

Featured Poets
Alok Kumar Ray * Eden S. Trinidad
Franco Barbato * Izabela Zubko

Ralph Bunche ~ 1950

The Year of Peace
Celebrating past Nobel Peace Prize Recipients

The Poetry Posse 2020

Gail Weston Shazor * Albert Carassco * Hülya N. Yılmaz
Jackie Davis Allen * Caroline Nazareno * Eliza Segiet
Alicja Maria Kuberska * Teresa E. Gallion * Joe Paire
Kimberly Burnham * Shareef Abdur – Rasheed
Ashok K. Bhargava * Elizabeth Castillo * Swapna Behera
Tezmin Ition Tsai * William S. Peters, Sr.

The Year of the Poet VII
June 2020

Featured Poets
Eftichia Kapardeli * Metin Cengiz
Hussein Habasch * Kosh K Mathew

Albert John Lutuli ~ 1960

The Year of Peace
Celebrating past Nobel Peace Prize Recipients

The Poetry Posse 2020

Gail Weston Shazor * Albert Carassco * Hülya N. Yılmaz
Jackie Davis Allen * Caroline Nazareno * Eliza Segiet
Alicja Maria Kuberska * Teresa E. Gallion * Joe Paire
Kimberly Burnham * Shareef Abdur – Rasheed
Ashok K. Bhargava * Elizabeth Castillo * Swapna Behera
Tezmin Ition Tsai * William S. Peters, Sr.

The Year of the Poet VII
July 2020

Featured Poets
Mykola Martyniuk * Orbindu Ganga
Roula Pollard * Kam Praktisha

Norman Ernest Borlaug ~ 1970

The Year of Peace
Celebrating past Nobel Peace Prize Recipients

The Poetry Posse 2020

Gail Weston Shazor * Albert Carassco * Hülya N. Yılmaz
Jackie Davis Allen * Caroline Nazareno * Eliza Segiet
Alicja Maria Kuberska * Teresa E. Gallion * Joe Paire
Kimberly Burnham * Shareef Abdur – Rasheed
Ashok K. Bhargava * Elizabeth Castillo * Swapna Behera
Tezmin Ition Tsai * William S. Peters, Sr.

The Year of the Poet VII
August 2020

Featured Poets
Dr Pragya Suman * Chinh Nguyen
Srinivas Vasudev * Ugwu Leonard Ifeanyi, Jr.

Adolfo Pérez Esquivel ~ 1980

The Year of Peace
Celebrating past Nobel Peace Prize Recipients

The Poetry Posse 2020

Gail Weston Shazor * Albert Carassco * Hülya N. Yılmaz
Jackie Davis Allen * Caroline Nazareno * Eliza Segiet
Alicja Maria Kuberska * Teresa E. Gallion * Joe Paire
Kimberly Burnham * Shareef Abdur – Rasheed
Ashok K. Bhargava * Elizabeth Castillo * Swapna Behera
Tezmin Ition Tsai * William S. Peters, Sr.

Now Available

www.innerchildpress.com/the-year-of-the-poet

The Year of the Poet VII

September 2020

Featured Poets

Raed Anis Al-Jishi • Sofkonović Snežana
Dr. Brajesh Kumar Gupta • Umid Najjari

Mikhail Sergeyevich Gorbachev ~ 1990

The Year of Peace
Celebrating past Nobel Peace Prize Recipients

The Poetry Posse 2020

Gail Weston Shazor • Albert Carasico • Hülya N. Yılmaz
Jackie Davis Allen • Caroline Nazareno • Eliza Segiet
Alicja Maria Kuberska • Teresa E. Gallion • Joe Paire
Kimberly Burnham • Shareef Abdur – Rasheed
Ashok K. Bhargava • Elizabeth Castillo • Swapna Behera
Tezmin Ition Tsai • William S. Peters, Sr.

The Year of the Poet VII

October 2020

Featured Poets

Mutawaf A. Shaheed • Galina Italyanskaya
Nadeem Fraz • Avril Tanya Meallem

Kim Dae-jung ~ 2000

The Year of Peace
Celebrating past Nobel Peace Prize Recipients

The Poetry Posse 2020

Gail Weston Shazor • Albert Carasico • Hülya N. Yılmaz
Jackie Davis Allen • Caroline Nazareno • Eliza Segiet
Alicja Maria Kuberska • Teresa E. Gallion • Joe Paire
Kimberly Burnham • Shareef Abdur – Rasheed
Ashok K. Bhargava • Elizabeth Castillo • Swapna Behera
Tezmin Ition Tsai • William S. Peters, Sr.

The Year of the Poet VII

November 2020

Featured Poets

Elisa Mascia • Sue Lindenberg McClelland
Hatif Janabi • Ivan Gaćina

Liu Xiaobo ~ 2010

The Year of Peace
Celebrating past Nobel Peace Prize Recipients

The Poetry Posse 2020

Gail Weston Shazor • Albert Carasico • Hülya N. Yılmaz
Jackie Davis Allen • Caroline Nazareno • Eliza Segiet
Alicja Maria Kuberska • Teresa E. Gallion • Joe Paire
Kimberly Burnham • Shareef Abdur – Rasheed
Ashok K. Bhargava • Elizabeth Castillo • Swapna Behera
Tezmin Ition Tsai • William S. Peters, Sr.

The Year of the Poet VII

December 2020

Featured Poets

Ratan Ghosh • Ibtisam Ibrahim Al-Asady
Brindha Vinodh • Selma Kopic

Abiy Ahmed Ali ~ 2019

The Year of Peace
Celebrating past Nobel Peace Prize Recipients

The Poetry Posse 2020

Gail Weston Shazor • Albert Carasico • Hülya N. Yılmaz
Jackie Davis Allen • Caroline Nazareno • Eliza Segiet
Alicja Maria Kuberska • Teresa E. Gallion • Joe Paire
Kimberly Burnham • Shareef Abdur – Rasheed
Ashok K. Bhargava • Elizabeth Castillo • Swapna Behera
Tezmin Ition Tsai • William S. Peters, Sr.

Now Available

www.innerchildpress.com/the-year-of-the-poet

The Year of the Poet VIII
January 2021

Featured Global Poets
Andrew Scott * Debaprasanna Biswas
Shakil Kalam * Changming Yuan

Banksy's The Girl with the Pierced Eardrum

Poetry . . . Ekphrasticly Speaking
The Poetry Posse 2020
Gail Weston Shazor * Albert Carasco * Hülya N. Yılmaz
Jackie Davis Allen * Caroline Nazareno * Eliza Segiet
Alicja Maria Kuberska * Teresa E. Gallion * Joe Paire
Kimberly Burnham * Shareef Abdur – Rasheed
Ashok K. Bhargava * Elizabeth Castillo * Swapna Behera
Tezmin Ition Tsai * William S. Peters, Sr.

The Year of the Poet VIII
February 2021

Featured Global Poets
T. Ramesh Babu * Ruchida Barman
Neptune Barman * Faleeha Hassan

Emory Douglas : 1968 Olympics mural

Poetry . . . Ekphrasticly Speaking
The Poetry Posse 2021
Gail Weston Shazor * Albert Carasco * Hülya N. Yılmaz
Jackie Davis Allen * Caroline Nazareno * Eliza Segiet
Alicja Maria Kuberska * Teresa E. Gallion * Joe Paire
Kimberly Burnham * Shareef Abdur – Rasheed
Ashok K. Bhargava * Elizabeth Castillo * Swapna Behera
Tezmin Ition Tsai * William S. Peters, Sr.

The Year of the Poet VIII
March 2021

Featured Global Poets
Claudia Piccinno * Mohammed Jabr
Luzviminda Rivera *Nigar Arif

Tatyana Fazlalizadeh

Poetry . . . Ekphrasticly Speaking
The Poetry Posse 2021
Gail Weston Shazor * Albert Carasco * Hülya N. Yılmaz
Jackie Davis Allen * Caroline Nazareno * Eliza Segiet
Alicja Maria Kuberska * Teresa E. Gallion * Joe Paire
Kimberly Burnham * Shareef Abdur – Rasheed
Ashok K. Bhargava * Elizabeth Castillo * Swapna Behera
Tezmin Ition Tsai * William S. Peters, Sr.

The Year of the Poet VIII
April 2021

Featured Global Poets
Katarzyna Brus- Sawczuk * Anwesha Paul
Rozalia Aleksandrova * Shahid Abbas

Pablo O'Higgins

Poetry . . . Ekphrasticly Speaking
The Poetry Posse 2021
Gail Weston Shazor * Albert Carasco * Hülya N. Yılmaz
Jackie Davis Allen * Caroline Nazareno * Eliza Segiet
Alicja Maria Kuberska * Teresa E. Gallion * Joe Paire
Kimberly Burnham * Shareef Abdur – Rasheed
Ashok K. Bhargava * Elizabeth Castillo * Swapna Behera
Tezmin Ition Tsai * William S. Peters, Sr.

Now Available

www.innerchildpress.com/the-year-of-the-poet

The Year of the Poet VIII
May 2021

Featured Global Poets
Paramita Mukherjee Mullick * Rose Zerguine
Jirydeep Sarangi * Brsmay Mohanty

Diego Rivera

Poetry ... Ekphrasticly Speaking
The Poetry Posse 2021
Gail Weston Shazor * Albert Carasco * Hülya N. Yılmaz
Jackie Davis Allen * Caroline Nazareno * Eliza Segiet
Alicja Maria Kuberska * Teresa E. Gallion * Joe Paire
Kimberly Burnham * Shareef Abdur – Rasheed
Ashok K. Bhargava * Elizabeth Castillo * Swapna Behera
Tezmin Ition Tsai * William S. Peters, Sr.

The Year of the Poet VIII
June 2021

Featured Global Poets
Alonzo "zO" Gross * Lali Tsipi Michaeli
Tareq al Karmy * Tirthendu Ganguly

Rayen Kang

Poetry ... Ekphrasticly Speaking
The Poetry Posse 2021
Gail Weston Shazor * Albert Carasco * Hülya N. Yılmaz
Jackie Davis Allen * Caroline Nazareno * Eliza Segiet
Alicja Maria Kuberska * Teresa E. Gallion * Joe Paire
Kimberly Burnham * Shareef Abdur – Rasheed
Ashok K. Bhargava * Elizabeth Castillo * Swapna Behera
Tezmin Ition Tsai * William S. Peters, Sr.

The Year of the Poet VIII
July 2021

Featured Global Poets
Iram Jaan * Vesna Mundishevska-Veljanovska
Ngozi Olivia Osuoha * Lan Qyqalla

Goncalao Mabunda

Poetry ... Ekphrasticly Speaking
The Poetry Posse 2021
Gail Weston Shazor * Albert Carasco * Hülya N. Yılmaz
Jackie Davis Allen * Caroline Nazareno * Eliza Segiet
Alicja Maria Kuberska * Teresa E. Gallion * Joe Paire
Kimberly Burnham * Shareef Abdur – Rasheed
Ashok K. Bhargava * Elizabeth Castillo * Swapna Behera
Tezmin Ition Tsai * William S. Peters, Sr.

The Year of the Poet VIII
August 2021

Featured Global Poets
Caroline Laurent Turunc * Kamal Dhungana
Pankhuri Sinha * Paramita Mukherjee Mullick

Mundara Koorang

Poetry ... Ekphrasticly Speaking
The Poetry Posse 2021
Gail Weston Shazor * Albert Carasco * Hülya N. Yılmaz
Jackie Davis Allen * Caroline Nazareno * Eliza Segiet
Alicja Maria Kuberska * Teresa E. Gallion * Joe Paire
Kimberly Burnham * Shareef Abdur – Rasheed
Ashok K. Bhargava * Elizabeth Castillo * Swapna Behera
Tezmin Ition Tsai * William S. Peters, Sr.

Now Available

www.innerchildpress.com/the-year-of-the-poet

The Year of the Poet VIII

September 2021

Featured Global Poets

Monsif Beroual * Sandesh Ghimire

Sharmila Poudel * Pavol Janik

Heather Jansch

Poetry . . . Ekphrasticly Speaking

The Poetry Posse 2021

Gail Weston Shazor * Albert Carasco * Hülya N. Yılmaz
Jackie Davis Allen * Caroline Nazareno * Eliza Segiet
Alicja Maria Kuberska * Teresa E. Gallion * Joe Paire
Kimberly Burnham * Shareef Abdur – Rasheed
Ashok K. Bhargava * Elizabeth Castillo * Swapna Behera
Tezmin Ition Tsai * William S. Peters, Sr.

The Year of the Poet VIII

October 2021

Featured Global Poets

C. E. Shy * Saswata Ganguly

Suranjit Gain * Hasiba Hilal

Dale Lamphere

Poetry . . . Ekphrasticly Speaking

The Poetry Posse 2021

Gail Weston Shazor * Albert Carasco * Hülya N. Yılmaz
Jackie Davis Allen * Caroline Nazareno * Eliza Segiet
Alicja Maria Kuberska * Teresa E. Gallion * Joe Paire
Kimberly Burnham * Shareef Abdur – Rasheed
Ashok K. Bhargava * Elizabeth Castillo * Swapna Behera
Tezmin Ition Tsai * William S. Peters, Sr.

The Year of the Poet VIII

November 2021

Featured Global Poets

Errol D. Bean * Ibrahim Honjo

Tanja Ajtic * Rajashree Mohapatra

Andy Goldsworthy

Poetry . . . Ekphrasticly Speaking

The Poetry Posse 2021

Gail Weston Shazor * Albert Carasco * Hülya N. Yılmaz
Jackie Davis Allen * Caroline Nazareno * Eliza Segiet
Alicja Maria Kuberska * Teresa E. Gallion * Joe Paire
Kimberly Burnham * Shareef Abdur – Rasheed
Ashok K. Bhargava * Elizabeth Castillo * Swapna Behera
Tezmin Ition Tsai * William S. Peters, Sr.

The Year of the Poet VIII

December 2021

Featured Global Poets

Orbinda Ganga * Fadairo Tesleem

Anthony Arnold * Iyad Shamasnah

Fredric Edwin Church

Poetry . . . Ekphrasticly Speaking

The Poetry Posse 2021

Gail Weston Shazor * Albert Carasco * Hülya N. Yılmaz
Jackie Davis Allen * Caroline Nazareno * Eliza Segiet
Alicja Maria Kuberska * Teresa E. Gallion * Joe Paire
Kimberly Burnham * Shareef Abdur – Rasheed
Ashok K. Bhargava * Elizabeth Castillo * Swapna Behera
Tezmin Ition Tsai * William S. Peters, Sr.

Now Available

www.innerchildpress.com/the-year-of-the-poet

The Year of the Poet IX
January 2022

Featured Global Poets
**Ratan Ghosh * Christine Neil-Wright
Andrew Scott * Ashok Kumar**

Climate Change : The Ice Cap

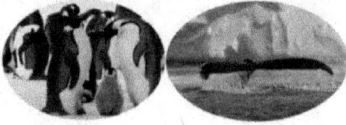

Poetry . . . Ekphrasticly Speaking

The Poetry Posse 2021

Gail Weston Shazor * Albert Carasco * Hülya N. Yılmaz
Jackie Davis Allen * Caroline Nazareno * Eliza Segiet
Alicja Maria Kuberska * Teresa E. Gallion * Joe Paire
Kimberly Burnham * Shareef Abdur – Rasheed
Ashok K. Bhargava * Elizabeth Castillo * Swapna Behera
Tezmin Ition Tsai * William S. Peters, Sr.

The Year of the Poet IX
February 2022

Featured Global Poets
Roza Boyanova * Ramón de Jesús Núñez Duval
Mammad Ismayil * Tarana Turan Rahimli

Climate Change and Mountains

Poetry . . . Ekphrasticly Speaking

The Poetry Posse 2021

Gail Weston Shazor * Albert Carasco * Hülya N. Yılmaz
Jackie Davis Allen * Caroline Nazareno * Eliza Segiet
Alicja Maria Kuberska * Teresa E. Gallion * Joe Paire
Kimberly Burnham * Shareef Abdur – Rasheed
Ashok K. Bhargava * Elizabeth Castillo * Swapna Behera
Tezmin Ition Tsai * William S. Peters, Sr.

The Year of the Poet IX
March 2022

Featured Global Poets
Dimitris P. Kraniotis * Marlene Pasini
Kennedy Ochieng * Swayam Prashant

Climate Change and Space Debris

Poetry . . . Ekphrasticly Speaking

The Poetry Posse 2021

Gail Weston Shazor * Albert Carasco * Hülya N. Yılmaz
Jackie Davis Allen * Caroline Nazareno * Eliza Segiet
Alicja Maria Kuberska * Teresa E. Gallion * Joe Paire
Kimberly Burnham * Shareef Abdur – Rasheed
Ashok K. Bhargava * Elizabeth Castillo * Swapna Behera
Tezmin Ition Tsai * William S. Peters, Sr.

The Year of the Poet IX
April 2022

Featured Global Poets
**Alonzo Gross * Dr. Debaprasanna Biswas
Monsif Beroual * Carol Aronoff**

Climate Change and Oceans

*Celebrating our 100th Edition *

Poetry . . . Ekphrasticly Speaking

The Poetry Posse 2021

Gail Weston Shazor * Albert Carasco * Hülya N. Yılmaz
Jackie Davis Allen * Caroline Nazareno * Eliza Segiet
Alicja Maria Kuberska * Teresa E. Gallion * Joe Paire
Kimberly Burnham * Shareef Abdur – Rasheed
Ashok K. Bhargava * Elizabeth Castillo * Swapna Behera
Tezmin Ition Tsai * William S. Peters, Sr.

Now Available

www.innerchildpress.com/the-year-of-the-poet

The Year of the Poet IX
May 2022

Featured Global Poets

Ndaba Sibanda * Smrutiranjan Mohanty
Ajanta Paul * Monalisa Dash Dwibedy

Climate Change and Birds

Poetry . . . Ekphrasticly Speaking

The Poetry Posse 2021

Gail Weston Shazor * Albert Carasco * Hülya N. Yılmaz
Jackie Davis Allen * Caroline Nazareno * Eliza Segiet
Alicja Maria Kuberska * Teresa E. Gallion * Joe Paire
Kimberly Burnham * Shareef Abdur – Rasheed
Ashok K. Bhargava * Elizabeth Castillo * Swapna Behera
Tezmin Ition Tsai * William S. Peters, Sr.

The Year of the Poet IX
June 2022

Featured Global Poets

Yuan Changming * Azeezat Okunlola
Tanja Ajtić * Philip Chijioke Abonyi

Climate Change and Trees

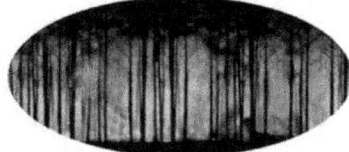

Poetry . . . Ekphrasticly Speaking

The Poetry Posse 2022

Gail Weston Shazor * Albert Carasco * Hülya N. Yılmaz
Jackie Davis Allen * Caroline Nazareno * Eliza Segiet
Alicja Maria Kuberska * Teresa E. Gallion * Joe Paire
Kimberly Burnham * Shareef Abdur – Rasheed
Ashok K. Bhargava * Elizabeth Castillo * Swapna Behera
Tezmin Ition Tsai * William S. Peters, Sr.

The Year of the Poet IX
July 2022

Featured Global Poets

Michelle Joan Barulich * Mili Das
Anna Ferriero * Ujjal Mandal

Climate Change and Animals

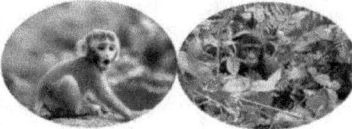

Poetry . . . Ekphrasticly Speaking

The Poetry Posse 2022

Gail Weston Shazor * Albert Carasco * Hülya N. Yılmaz
Jackie Davis Allen * Caroline Nazareno * Eliza Segiet
Alicja Maria Kuberska * Teresa E. Gallion * Joe Paire
Kimberly Burnham * Shareef Abdur – Rasheed
Ashok K. Bhargava * Elizabeth Castillo * Swapna Behera
Tezmin Ition Tsai * William S. Peters, Sr.

The Year of the Poet IX
August 2022

Featured Global Poets

Pankhuri Sinha * Abdulloh Abdumominov
Caroline Turunç * Tali Cohen Shabtai

Climate Change and Agriculture

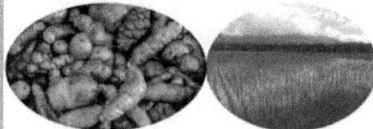

Poetry . . . Ekphrasticly Speaking

The Poetry Posse 2022

Gail Weston Shazor * Albert Carasco * Hülya N. Yılmaz
Jackie Davis Allen * Caroline Nazareno * Eliza Segiet
Alicja Maria Kuberska * Teresa E. Gallion * Joe Paire
Kimberly Burnham * Shareef Abdur – Rasheed
Ashok K. Bhargava * Elizabeth Castillo * Swapna Behera
Tezmin Ition Tsai * William S. Peters, Sr.

Now Available

www.innerchildpress.com/the-year-of-the-poet

The Year of the Poet IX
September 2022

Featured Global Poets

Ngozi Olivia Osuoba * Biswajit Mishra
Sylwia K. Malinowska * Sajid Hussein

Climate Change and Wind and Weather Patterns

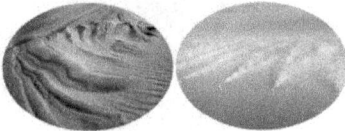

Poetry . . . Ekphrasticly Speaking

The Poetry Posse 2022

Gail Weston Shazor * Albert Carasco * Hülya N. Yılmaz
Jackie Davis Allen * Caroline Nazareno * Eliza Segiet
Alicja Maria Kuberska * Teresa E. Gallion * Joe Paire
Kimberly Burnham * Shareef Abdur – Rasheed
Ashok K. Bhargava * Elizabeth Castillo * Swapna Behera
Tezmin Ition Tsai * William S. Peters, Sr.

The Year of the Poet IX
October 2022

Featured Global Poets

Andrew Kouroupos * Brenda Mohammed
Carthornia Kouroupos * Faleeha Hassan

Climate Change and Oil and Power

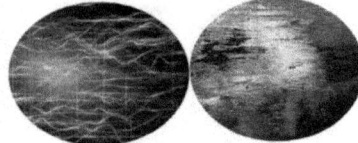

Poetry . . . Ekphrasticly Speaking

The Poetry Posse 2022

Gail Weston Shazor * Albert Carasco * Hülya N. Yılmaz
Jackie Davis Allen * Caroline Nazareno * Eliza Segiet
Alicja Maria Kuberska * Teresa E. Gallion * Joe Paire
Kimberly Burnham * Shareef Abdur – Rasheed
Ashok K. Bhargava * Elizabeth Castillo * Swapna Behera
Tezmin Ition Tsai * William S. Peters, Sr.

The Year of the Poet IX
November 2022

Featured Global Poets

Hema Ravi * Shafkat Aziz Hajam
Selma Kopic * Ibrahim Honjo

Climate Change : Time to Act

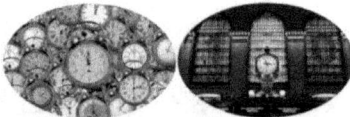

Poetry . . . Ekphrasticly Speaking

The Poetry Posse 2022

Gail Weston Shazor * Albert Carasco * Hülya N. Yılmaz
Jackie Davis Allen * Caroline Nazareno * Eliza Segiet
Alicja Maria Kuberska * Teresa E. Gallion * Joe Paire
Kimberly Burnham * Shareef Abdur – Rasheed
Ashok K. Bhargava * Elizabeth Castillo * Swapna Behera
Tezmin Ition Tsai * William S. Peters, Sr.

The Year of the Poet IX
December 2022

Featured Global Poets

Elarbi Abdelfattah * Lorraine Cragg
Neha Bhandarkar * Robert Gibbons

Climate Change Bees, Butterflies and Insect Life

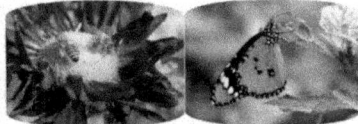

Poetry . . . Ekphrasticly Speaking

The Poetry Posse 2022

Gail Weston Shazor * Albert Carasco * Hülya N. Yılmaz
Jackie Davis Allen * Caroline Nazareno * Eliza Segiet
Alicja Maria Kuberska * Teresa E. Gallion * Joe Paire
Kimberly Burnham * Shareef Abdur – Rasheed
Ashok K. Bhargava * Elizabeth Castillo * Swapna Behera
Tezmin Ition Tsai * William S. Peters, Sr.

Now Available

www.innerchildpress.com/the-year-of-the-poet

The Year of the Poet X
January 2023

Featured Global Poets

JuNe Barefield * Swayam Prashant
Willow Rose * Shabbirhusein K Jamnagerwalla

Children : Difference Makers

Iqbal Masih

The Poetry Posse 2023

Gail Weston Shazor * Albert Carasco * Hülya N. Yılmaz
Jackie Davis Allen * Caroline Nazareno * Kimberly Burnham
Alicja Maria Kuberska * Teresa E. Gallion * Joe Paire
Michelle Joan Barulich * Shareef Abdur – Rasheed
Ashok K. Bhargava * Elizabeth Castillo * Swapna Behera
Tezmin Ition Tsai * Eliza Segiet * William S. Peters, Sr.

The Year of the Poet X
February 2023

Featured Global Poets

Christena Williams * Hilda Graciela Kraft
Francesco Favetta * Dr. H.C. Louise Hudon

Children : Difference Makers

Ruby Bridges

The Poetry Posse 2023

Gail Weston Shazor * Albert Carasco * Hülya N. Yılmaz
Jackie Davis Allen * Caroline Nazareno * Kimberly Burnham
Alicja Maria Kuberska * Teresa E. Gallion * Joe Paire
Michelle Joan Barulich * Shareef Abdur – Rasheed
Ashok K. Bhargava * Elizabeth Castillo * Swapna Behera
Tezmin Ition Tsai * Eliza Segiet * William S. Peters, Sr.

The Year of the Poet X
March 2023

Featured Global Poets

Clarena Martinez Turizo * Binod Dawadi
Til Kumari Sharma * Petrouchka Alexieva

Children : Difference Makers

Yo Yo Ma

The Poetry Posse 2023

Gail Weston Shazor * Albert Carasco * Hülya N. Yılmaz
Jackie Davis Allen * Caroline Nazareno * Kimberly Burnham
Alicja Maria Kuberska * Teresa E. Gallion * Joe Paire
Michelle Joan Barulich * Shareef Abdur – Rasheed
Ashok K. Bhargava * Elizabeth Castillo * Swapna Behera
Tezmin Ition Tsai * Eliza Segiet * William S. Peters, Sr.

The Year of the Poet X
April 2023

Featured Global Poets

Maxwanette A Poetess * Alonzo Gross
Türkan Ergör * Ibrahim Honjo

Children : Difference Makers

Claudette Colvin

The Poetry Posse 2023

Gail Weston Shazor * Albert Carasco * Hülya N. Yılmaz
Jackie Davis Allen * Caroline Nazareno * Kimberly Burnham
Alicja Maria Kuberska * Teresa E. Gallion * Joe Paire
Michelle Joan Barulich * Shareef Abdur – Rasheed
Ashok K. Bhargava * Elizabeth Castillo * Swapna Behera
Tezmin Ition Tsai * Eliza Segiet * William S. Peters, Sr.

Now Available

www.innerchildpress.com/the-year-of-the-poet

The Year of the Poet X
May 2023

Csp Shrivastava * Michael Lee Johnson
Taghrid Bou Merhi * Yasmin Brown

Children : Difference Makers

Louis Braille
The Poetry Posse 2023

Gail Weston Shazor * Albert Carasico * Hülya N. Yilmaz
Jackie Davis Allen * Caroline Nazareno * Kimberly Burnham
Alicja Maria Kuberska * Teresa E. Gallion * Joe Paire
Michelle Joan Barulich * Shareef Abdur – Rasheed
Ashok K. Bhargava * Elizabeth Castillo * Swapna Behera
Tezmin Ition Tsai * Eliza Segiet * William S. Peters, Sr.

The Year of the Poet X
June 2023

Featured Global Poets

Kay Peters · Carthornia Kouroupos
Andrew Kouroupos · Faleeha Hassan

Children : Difference Makers

Ryan Hreljac
The Poetry Posse 2023

Gail Weston Shazor * Albert Carasico * Hülya N. Yilmaz
Jackie Davis Allen * Caroline Nazareno * Kimberly Burnham
Alicja Maria Kuberska * Teresa E. Gallion * Joe Paire
Michelle Joan Barulich * Shareef Abdur – Rasheed
Ashok K. Bhargava * Elizabeth Castillo * Swapna Behera
Tezmin Ition Tsai * Eliza Segiet * William S. Peters, Sr.

The Year of the Poet X
July 2023

Featured Global Poets

Rajashree Mohapatra * Biswajit Mishra
Johan Karlsson * Teodozja Swiderska

Children : Difference Makers

~ Bana al-Abed ~
The Poetry Posse 2023

Gail Weston Shazor * Albert Carasico * Hülya N. Yilmaz
Jackie Davis Allen * Caroline Nazareno * Kimberly Burnham
Alicja Maria Kuberska * Teresa E. Gallion * Joe Paire
Michelle Joan Barulich * Shareef Abdur – Rasheed
Ashok K. Bhargava * Elizabeth Castillo * Swapna Behera
Tezmin Ition Tsai * Eliza Segiet * William S. Peters, Sr.

The Year of the Poet X
August 2023

Featured Global Poets

Kennedy Wanda Ochieng * Jose Lopez
Sylwia K. Malinowska * Laurent Grison

Children : Difference Makers

~ Kelvin Doe ~
The Poetry Posse 2023

Gail Weston Shazor * Albert Carasico * Hülya N. Yilmaz
Jackie Davis Allen * Caroline Nazareno * Kimberly Burnham
Alicja Maria Kuberska * Teresa E. Gallion * Joe Paire
Michelle Joan Barulich * Shareef Abdur – Rasheed
Ashok K. Bhargava * Elizabeth Castillo * Swapna Behera
Tezmin Ition Tsai * Eliza Segiet * William S. Peters, Sr.

Now Available

www.innerchildpress.com/the-year-of-the-poet

The Year of the Poet X
September 2023

Featured Global Poets

Eftichia Karpadeli * Chinh Nguyen
Nigar Agalarova * Carmela Cueva

Children : Difference Makers

~ Easton LaChappelle ~
The Poetry Posse 2023

Gail Weston Shazor * Albert Carasco * Hülya N. Yılmaz
Jackie Davis Allen * Caroline Nazareno * Kimberly Burnham
Alicja Maria Kuberska * Teresa E. Gallion * Joe Paire
Michelle Joan Barulich * Shareef Abdur – Rasheed
Ashok K. Bhargava * Elizabeth Castillo * Swapna Behera
Tezmin Ition Tsai * Eliza Segiet * William S. Peters, Sr.

The Year of the Poet X
October 2023

Featured Global Poets

CSP Shrivastava * Huniie Parker
Noreen Snyder * Ramkrishna Paul

Children : Difference Makers

~ Malala Yousafzai ~
The Poetry Posse 2023

Gail Weston Shazor * Albert Carasco * Hülya N. Yılmaz
Jackie Davis Allen * Caroline Nazareno * Kimberly Burnham
Alicja Maria Kuberska * Teresa E. Gallion * Joe Paire
Michelle Joan Barulich * Shareef Abdur – Rasheed
Ashok K. Bhargava * Elizabeth Castillo * Swapna Behera
Tezmin Ition Tsai * Eliza Segiet * William S. Peters, Sr.

The Year of the Poet X
November 2023

Featured Global Poets

Ibrahim Honjo * Balachandran Nair
Xanthi Hondrou-Hil * Francesco Favetta

Children : Difference Makers

~ Jean-Michel Basquiat ~
The Poetry Posse 2023

Gail Weston Shazor * Albert Carasco * Hülya N. Yılmaz
Jackie Davis Allen * Caroline Nazareno * Kimberly Burnham
Alicja Maria Kuberska * Teresa E. Gallion * Joe Paire
Michelle Joan Barulich * Shareef Abdur – Rasheed
Ashok K. Bhargava * Elizabeth Castillo * Swapna Behera
Tezmin Ition Tsai * Eliza Segiet * William S. Peters, Sr.

The Year of the Poet X
December 2023

Featured Global Poets

Caroline Laurent Turunc * Neha Bhandarkar
Shafkat Aziz Hajam * Elarbi Abdelfattah

Children : Difference Makers

~ Melati and Isabel Wijsen ~
The Poetry Posse 2023

Gail Weston Shazor * Albert Carasco * Hülya N. Yılmaz
Jackie Davis Allen * Caroline Nazareno * Kimberly Burnham
Alicja Maria Kuberska * Teresa E. Gallion * Joe Paire
Michelle Joan Barulich * Shareef Abdur – Rasheed
Ashok K. Bhargava * Elizabeth Castillo * Swapna Behera
Tezmin Ition Tsai * Eliza Segiet * William S. Peters, Sr.

Now Available

www.innerchildpress.com/the-year-of-the-poet

The Year of the Poet XI
January 2024

Featured Global Poets

Til Kumari Sharma * Shafkat Aziz Hajam
Daniela Marian * Eleni Vassiliou – Asteroskon

Renowned Poets

~ Phyllis Wheatley ~

The Poetry Posse 2024

Gail Weston Shazor * Albert Carasco * Hülya N. Yılmaz
Jackie Davis Allen * Caroline Nazareno * Mutawaf Shaheed
Alicja Maria Kuberska * Teresa E. Gallion * Noreen Snyder
Michelle Joan Barulich * Shareef Abdur – Rasheed
Ashok K. Bhargava * Elizabeth Castillo * Swapna Behera
Tezmin Ition Tsai * Eliza Segiet * William S. Peters, Sr.

The Year of the Poet XI
February 2024

Featured Global Poets

Caroline Laurent Turunç * Julio Pavanetti
Lidia Chiarelli * Lina Buividavičiūtė

Renowned Poets

~ Omar Khayyam ~

The Poetry Posse 2024

Gail Weston Shazor * Albert Carasco * Hülya N. Yılmaz
Jackie Davis Allen * Caroline Nazareno * Mutawaf Shaheed
Alicja Maria Kuberska * Teresa E. Gallion * Noreen Snyder
Michelle Joan Barulich * Shareef Abdur – Rasheed
Ashok K. Bhargava * Elizabeth Castillo * Swapna Behera
Tezmin Ition Tsai * Eliza Segiet * William S. Peters, Sr.

The Year of the Poet XI
March 2024

Featured Global Poets

Francesco Favetta * Jagjit Singh Zandu
Carmela Núñez Yukimura Peruana * Michael Lee Johnson

Renowned Poets

~ Nâzim Hikmet ~

The Poetry Posse 2024

Gail Weston Shazor * Albert Carasco * Hülya N. Yılmaz
Jackie Davis Allen * Caroline Nazareno * Mutawaf Shaheed
Alicja Maria Kuberska * Teresa E. Gallion * Noreen Snyder
Michelle Joan Barulich * Shareef Abdur – Rasheed
Ashok K. Bhargava * Elizabeth Castillo * Swapna Behera
Tezmin Ition Tsai * Eliza Segiet * William S. Peters, Sr.

The Year of the Poet XI
April 2024

Featured Global Poets

Hassanal Abdullah * Johny Takkedasila
Rajashree Mohapatra * Shirley Smothers

Renowned Poets

~ William Butler Yeats ~

The Poetry Posse 2024

Gail Weston Shazor * Albert Carasco * Hülya N. Yılmaz
Jackie Davis Allen * Caroline Nazareno * Mutawaf Shaheed
Alicja Maria Kuberska * Teresa E. Gallion * Noreen Snyder
Michelle Joan Barulich * Shareef Abdur – Rasheed
Ashok K. Bhargava * Elizabeth Castillo * Swapna Behera
Tezmin Ition Tsai * Eliza Segiet * William S. Peters, Sr.

Now Available

www.innerchildpress.com/the-year-of-the-poet

The Year of the Poet XI
May 2024

Featured Global Poets

Binod Dawadi * Petros Kyriakou Veloudas
Rayees Ahmad Kumar * Solomon C Jatta

Renowned Poets

~ Makhanlal Chaturvedi ~

The Poetry Posse 2024

Gail Weston Shazor * Albert Carasco * Hülya N. Yılmaz
Jackie Davis Allen * Caroline Nazareno * Mutawaf Shaheed
Alicja Maria Kuberska * Teresa E. Gallion * Noreen Snyder
Michelle Joan Barulich * Shareef Abdur – Rasheed
Ashok K. Bhargava * Elizabeth Castillo * Swapna Behera
Tezmin Ition Tsai * Eliza Segiet * William S. Peters, Sr.

The Year of the Poet XI
June 2024

Featured Global Poets

C. S. P Shrivastava * Maria Evelyn Quilla Soleta
Moulay Cherif Chebihi Hassani * Swayam Prashant

Renowned Poets

~ Langston Hughs ~

The Poetry Posse 2024

Gail Weston Shazor * Albert Carasco * Hülya N. Yılmaz
Jackie Davis Allen * Caroline Nazareno * Mutawaf Shaheed
Alicja Maria Kuberska * Teresa E. Gallion * Noreen Snyder
Michelle Joan Barulich * Shareef Abdur – Rasheed
Ashok K. Bhargava * Elizabeth Castillo * Swapna Behera
Tezmin Ition Tsai * Eliza Segiet * William S. Peters, Sr.

The Year of the Poet XI
July 2024

Featured Global Poets

Barbara Gaiardoni * Bharati Nayak
Errol Bean * Michael Lee Johnson

Renowned Poets

~ Pablo Neruda ~

The Poetry Posse 2024

Gail Weston Shazor * Albert Carasco * Hülya N. Yılmaz
Jackie Davis Allen * Caroline Nazareno * Mutawaf Shaheed
Alicja Maria Kuberska * Teresa E. Gallion * Noreen Snyder
Michelle Joan Barulich * Shareef Abdur – Rasheed
Ashok K. Bhargava * Elizabeth Castillo * Swapna Behera
Tezmin Ition Tsai * Eliza Segiet * William S. Peters, Sr.

The Year of the Poet XI
August 2024

Featured Global Poets

Ibrahim Honjo * Khalice Jade
Irma Kurti * Mennadi Farah

Renowned Poets

~ Li Bai ~

The Poetry Posse 2024

Gail Weston Shazor * Albert Carasco * Hülya N. Yılmaz
Jackie Davis Allen * Caroline Nazareno * Mutawaf Shaheed
Alicja Maria Kuberska * Teresa E. Gallion * Noreen Snyder
Michelle Joan Barulich * Shareef Abdur – Rasheed
Ashok K. Bhargava * Elizabeth Castillo * Swapna Behera
Tezmin Ition Tsai * Eliza Segiet * William S. Peters, Sr.

Now Available

www.innerchildpress.com/the-year-of-the-poet

Inner Child Press Anthologies

The Year of the Poet XI
September 2024

Featured Global Poets

Ngozi Olivia Osuoha * Teodozja Świderska
Chinh Nguyen * Awatef El Idrissi Boukhris

Renowned Poets

~ William Ernest Henley ~
The Poetry Posse 2024

Gail Weston Shazor * Albert Carasco * Hülya N. Yılmaz
Jackie Davis Allen * Caroline Nazareno * Mutawaf Shaheed
Alicja Maria Kuberska * Teresa E. Gallion * Noreen Snyder
Michelle Joan Barulich * Shareef Abdur – Rasheed
Ashok K. Bhargava * Elizabeth Castillo * Swapna Behera
Tezmin Ition Tsai * Eliza Segiet * William S. Peters, Sr.

The Year of the Poet XI
October 2024

Featured Global Poets

Deepak Kumar Dey * Shallal 'Anouz
Adnan Al-Sayegh * Taghrid Bou Merhi

Renowned Poets

~ Adam Mickiewicz ~
The Poetry Posse 2024

Gail Weston Shazor * Albert Carasco * Hülya N. Yılmaz
Jackie Davis Allen * Caroline Nazareno * Mutawaf Shaheed
Alicja Maria Kuberska * Teresa E. Gallion * Noreen Snyder
Michelle Joan Barulich * Shareef Abdur – Rasheed
Ashok K. Bhargava * Elizabeth Castillo * Swapna Behera
Tezmin Ition Tsai * Eliza Segiet * William S. Peters, Sr.

The Year of the Poet XI
November 2024

Featured Global Poets

Abraham Tawiah Tei * Neha Bhandarkar
Zaneta Varnado Johns * Haseena Bnaiyan

Renowned Poets

~ Wole Soyinka ~
The Poetry Posse 2024

Gail Weston Shazor * Albert Carasco * Hülya N. Yılmaz
Jackie Davis Allen * Caroline Nazareno * Mutawaf Shaheed
Alicja Maria Kuberska * Teresa E. Gallion * Noreen Snyder
Michelle Joan Barulich * Shareef Abdur – Rasheed
Ashok K. Bhargava * Elizabeth Castillo * Swapna Behera
Tezmin Ition Tsai * Eliza Segiet * William S. Peters, Sr.

The Year of the Poet XI
December 2024

Featured Global Poets

Kapardeli Eftichia * Irena Jovanović
Sudipta Mishra * Til Kumari Sharma

Renowned Poets

~ Imru' al-Qais ~
The Poetry Posse 2024

Gail Weston Shazor * Albert Carasco * Hülya N. Yılmaz
Jackie Davis Allen * Caroline Nazareno * Mutawaf Shaheed
Alicja Maria Kuberska * Teresa E. Gallion * Noreen Snyder
Michelle Joan Barulich * Shareef Abdur – Rasheed
Ashok K. Bhargava * Elizabeth Castillo * Kimberly Burnham
Tezmin Ition Tsai * Eliza Segiet * William S. Peters, Sr.

Now Available

www.innerchildpress.com/the-year-of-the-poet

The Year of the Poet XII
January 2025

Featured Global Poets

Khalice Jade * Til Kumari Sharma
Sushant Thapa * Orbindu Ganga

 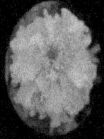 

| Innocence | Joy | Longing |
| Daisy | Marigold | Camellia |

The Poetry Posse 2025

Gail Weston Shazor * Albert Carasco * Hülya N. Yılmaz
Jackie Davis Allen * Caroline Nazareno * Mutawaf Shaheed
Alicja Maria Kuberska * Teresa E. Gallion * Noreen Snyder
Shareef Abdur – Rasheed * Swapna Behera * Eliza Segiet
Ashok K. Bhargava * Elizabeth Castillo * Kimberly Burnham
Tzemin Ition Tsai * William S. Peters, Sr.

The Year of the Poet XII
February 2025

Featured Global Poets

Shafkat Aziz Hajam * Frosina Tasevska
Muhammad Gaddafi Masoud * Karen Morrison

 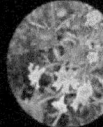 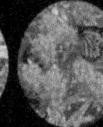

| Curiosity | Fear | Lonlines |
| Hibiscus | Minulus | Butterfly Weed |

The Poetry Posse 2025

Gail Weston Shazor * Albert Carasco * Hülya N. Yılmaz
Jackie Davis Allen * Caroline Nazareno * Mutawaf Shaheed
Alicja Maria Kuberska * Teresa E. Gallion * Noreen Snyder
Shareef Abdur – Rasheed * Swapna Behera * Eliza Segiet
Ashok K. Bhargava * Elizabeth Castillo * Kimberly Burnham
Tzemin Ition Tsai * William S. Peters, Sr.

The Year of the Poet XII
March 2025

Featured Global Poets

Deepak Kumar Dey * Binod Dawadi
Faleeha Hassan * Kapardeli Eftichia

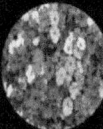 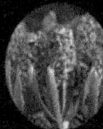 

| Frustration | Sorrow | Detrmination |
| Petunias | Purple Hyacinth | Amaryllis |

The Poetry Posse 2025

Gail Weston Shazor * Albert Carasco * Hülya N. Yılmaz
Jackie Davis Allen * Caroline Nazareno * Mutawaf Shaheed
Alicja Maria Kuberska * Teresa E. Gallion * Noreen Snyder
Shareef Abdur – Rasheed * Swapna Behera * Eliza Segiet
Ashok K. Bhargava * Elizabeth Castillo * Kimberly Burnham
Tzemin Ition Tsai * William S. Peters, Sr.

The Year of the Poet XII
April 2025

Featured Global Poets

Gopal Sinha * Taghrid Bou Merhi
Irma Kurti * Marlon Salem Gruezo

| Resilience | Self Doubt | Grief |
| Calendula | Centaury | Chrysanthemums |

The Poetry Posse 2025

Gail Weston Shazor * Albert Carasco * Hülya N. Yılmaz
Jackie Davis Allen * Caroline Nazareno * Mutawaf Shaheed
Alicja Maria Kuberska * Teresa E. Gallion * Noreen Snyder
Shareef Abdur – Rasheed * Swapna Behera * Eliza Segiet
Ashok K. Bhargava * Elizabeth Castillo * Kimberly Burnham
Tzemin Ition Tsai * William S. Peters, Sr.

Now Available

www.innerchildpress.com/the-year-of-the-poet

and there is much, much more !

visit . . .

www.innerchildpress.com/antho logies-sales-special.php

Also check out our Authors and all the wonderful Books Available at :

www.innerchildpress.com/autho rs-pages

World Healing
World Peace
2022

Poets for Humanity

Now Available

www.worldhealingworldpeacepoetry.com

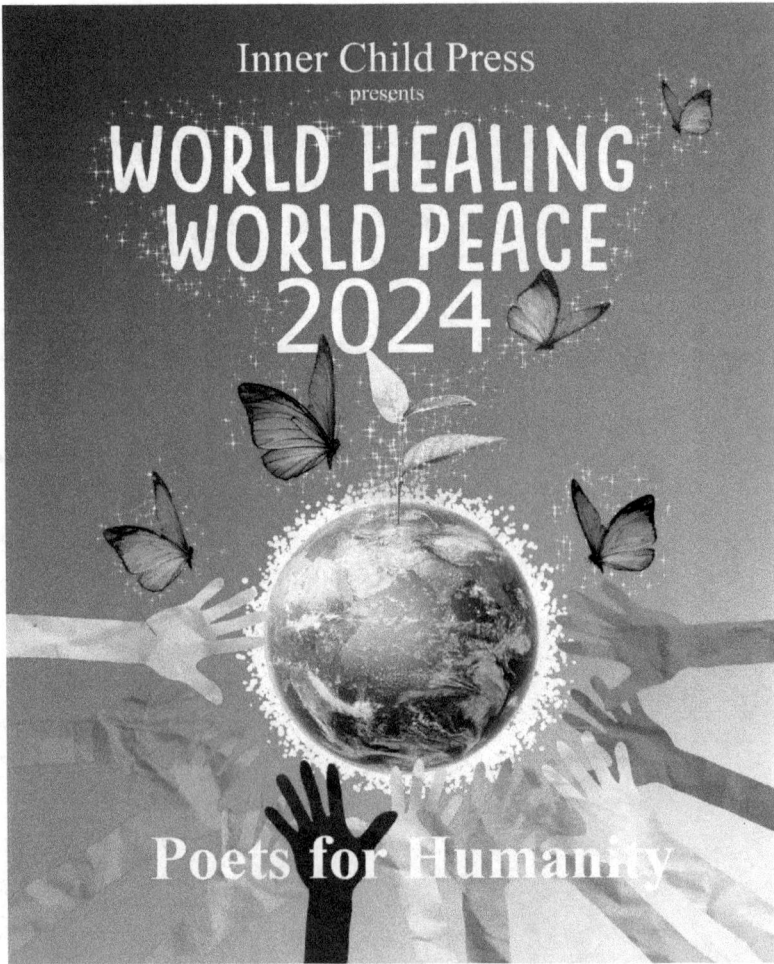

Inner Child Press
presents

WORLD HEALING
WORLD PEACE
2024

Poets for Humanity

Now Available

www.worldhealingworldpeacepoetry.com

World Healing World Peace 2020

Poets for Humanity

Now Available

www.worldhealingworldpeacepoetry.com

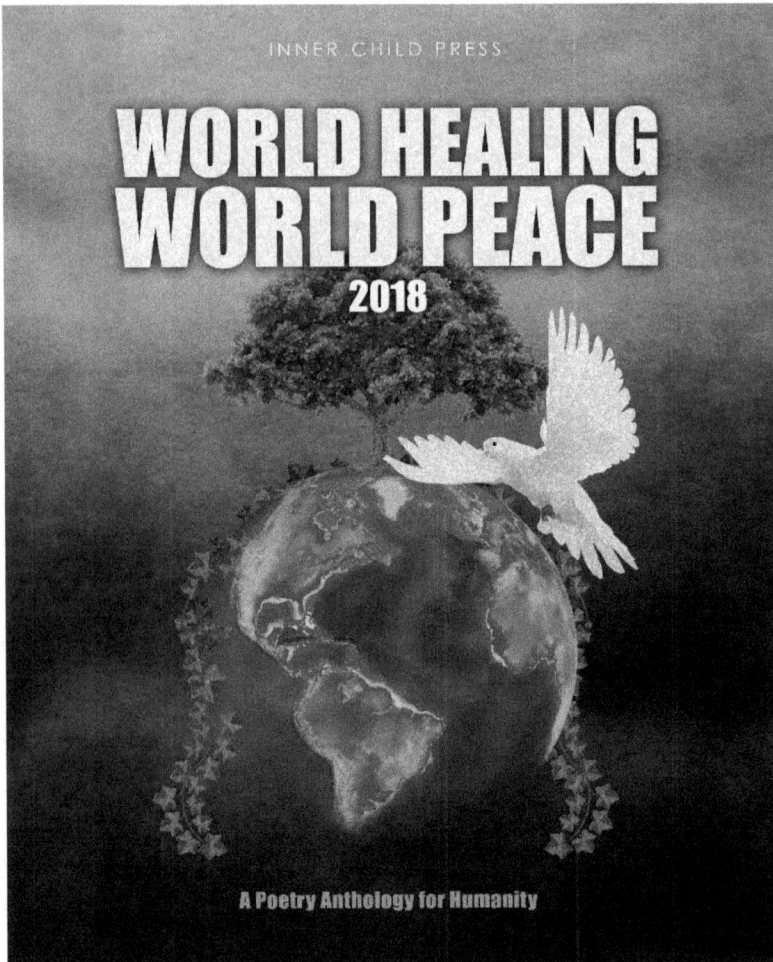

WORLD HEALING WORLD PEACE
2018

A Poetry Anthology for Humanity

Now Available

www.worldhealingworldpeacepoetry.com

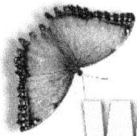

I support World Healing World Peace

www.worldhealingworldpeacepoetry.com

World Healing World Peace

World Healing World Peace

i am a believer !

World Healing
World Peace

2012, 2014, 2016, 2018,
2020, 2022, 2024

Now Available

www.worldhealingworldpeacepoetry.com

Inner Child Press International

'building bridges of cultural understanding'

Meet our Cultural Ambassadors

Fahredin Shehu
Director of Cultural

Faleha Hassan
Iraq – USA

Elizabeth E. Castillo
Philippines

Antoinette Coleman
Chicago
Midwest USA

Ananda Nepali
Nepal – Tibet
Northern India

Kimberly Burnham
Pacific Northwest
USA

Alicja Kuberska
Poland
Eastern Europe

Swapna Behera
India
Southeast Asia

Kolade O. Freedom
Nigeria
West Africa

Monsif Beroual
Morocco
Northern Africa

Ashok K. Bhargava
Canada

Tzemin Ition Tsai
Republic of China
Greater China

Alicia M. Ramírez
Mexico
Central America

Christena AV Williams
Jamaica
Caribbean

Louise Hudon
Eastern Canada

Aziz Mountassir
Morocco
Northern Africa

Shareef Abdur-Rasheed
Southeastern USA

Laure Charazac
France
Western Europe

Mohammad Ikbal Harb
Lebanon
Middle East

Mohamed Abdel
Aziz Shmeis
Egypt
Middle East

Hilary-Muinga
Kenya
Eastern Africa

Josephus R. Johnson
Liberia

Mennadi Farah
Algeria

www.innerchildpress.com

This Anthological Publication
is underwritten solely by

Inner Child Press International

Inner Child Press is a Publishing Company
Founded and Operated by Writers. Our
personal publishing experiences provides
us an intimate understanding of the
sometimes daunting challenges Writers,
New and Seasoned may face in the
Business of Publishing and Marketing
their Creative "Written Work".

For more Information

Inner Child Press International

www.innerchildpress.com

'building bridges of cultural understanding'
202 Wiltree Court, State College, Pennsylvania 16801

www.innerchildpress.com

~ *fini* ~